the answer
to how
is yes

the answer
to how

is yes

ACTING ON WHAT MATTERS

peter block

BK BERRETT-KOEHLER PUBLISHERS, INC.
San Francisco

Berrett-Koehler Publishers, Inc.
235 Montgomery Street, Suite 650
San Francisco, CA 94104-2916
Tel: (415) 288-0260   Fax: (415) 362-2512   www.bkconnection.com

ORDERING INFORMATION

Quantity sales. Special discounts are available on quantity purchases by corporations, associations, and others. For details, contact the "Special Sales Department" at the Berrett-Koehler address above.

Individual sales. Berrett-Koehler publications are available through most bookstores. They can also be ordered direct from Berrett-Koehler: Tel: (800) 929-2929; Fax: (802) 864-7626; www.bkconnection.com

Orders for college textbook/course adoption use. Please contact Berrett-Koehler: Tel: (800) 929-2929; Fax: (802) 864-7626.

Orders by U.S. trade bookstores and wholesalers. Please contact Publishers Group West, 1700 Fourth Street, Berkeley, CA 94710. Tel: (510) 528-1444; Fax (510) 528-3444.

 Printed in the United States of America
Printed on acid-free and recycled paper that is composed of 80% recovered fiber, including 30% post-consumer waste.

Library of Congress Cataloging-in-Publication Data

Block, Peter.
   The answer to how is yes : acting on what matters / Peter Block.
     p. cm.
   Includes bibliographical references and index.
   ISBN 1-57675-168-6
   1. Self-actualization (Psychology) I. Title.

BF637.S4 B572 2001
158.1--dc21

                               2001046071

First Edition

06 05 04 03 02   10 9 8 7 6 5 4 3 2

Developmental editor: Leslie Stephen

Copy editor: Veronica Randall

Photography by Jim Block

Rock balancing sculptures by Bill Dan

Cover designed by Mark van Bronkhorst, MvB Design

Text designed by Brad Greene, Greene Design

Dedication

To Jim,

with love and respect.

&

To Cathy, my muse.

Contents

▼

Transformation comes more from

pursuing profound questions

than seeking practical answers.

what
matters

introduction: acting on what matters.

There is depth in the question "How do I do this?" that is worth exploring. The question is a defense against the action. It is a leap past the question of purpose, past the question of intentions, and past the drama of responsibility. The question "How?"—more than any other question—looks for the answer outside of us. It is an indirect expression of our doubts. . . .

"Choosing Freedom, Service, and Adventure,"
—Peter Block, *Stewardship*, (p. 234)

There is something in the persistent question How? that expresses each person's struggle between having confidence in their capacity to live a life of purpose and yielding to the daily demands of being practical. It is entirely possible to spend our days engaged in activities that work well for us and achieve our objectives, and still wonder whether we are really making a difference in the world. My premise is that this culture, and we as members of it, have yielded too easily to what is doable and practical and popular. In the process we have sacrificed the pursuit of what is in our hearts. We find ourselves giving in to our doubts, and settling for what we know how to do, or can soon learn how to do, instead of pursuing what most matters to us and living with the adventure and anxiety that this requires.

The idea that asking how to do something may be an obstacle rather than an enabler ended my 1993 book, *Stewardship*. In the final chapter, there is the suggestion that How? is a symbol of our caution and reinforces the belief that, no matter what the question, there is an answer out there that I need and will make the difference. I pick How? as a symbol simply because it is far and away the most common question I hear. It has always struck me that I can write or speak the most radical thoughts imaginable. I can advocate revolution, the end of leadership, the abolition of appraising each other, the empowerment of the least among us, the end of life on the planet as we know it, and no one ever argues with me. The only questions I hear are "How do you get there from here? Where has this worked? What would it cost and what is the return on investment?" This has led me to the belief that the questions about How? are more interesting than any answer to them might be. They stand for some deeper concerns. So in this book, the starting point is to question the questions.

What Is Worth Doing

We often avoid the question of whether something is worth doing by going straight to the question "How do we do it?" In fact, when we believe that something is definitely not worth doing, we are particularly eager to start asking How? We can look at what is worth doing at many different levels: As an individual I can wonder whether I can be myself and do what I want and still make a living. For an organization I can ask for whose sake does this organization exist and does it exist for any larger purpose than to survive and be economically successful? As a society, have we replaced a sense of community and civic engagement for economic well being and the pursuit of our private ambition?

Too often when a discussion is dominated by questions of How? we risk overvaluing what is practical and doable and postpone the questions of larger purpose and collective well being. With the question How? we risk aspiring to goals that are defined for us by the culture and by our institutions, at the expense of pursuing purposes and intentions that arise from within ourselves.

If we were really committed to the pursuit of what matters, we might be well served to hold a moratorium on the question How? There is an image I first heard from Jim Walker, a change-oriented executive and good soul, who was put in charge of a struggling AT&T business some years ago. He used to ask, "What do you do when you find yourself in a hole?" His answer was, "The first thing you do is stop digging." That stuck with me. Most of the time, when something I am trying does not work, I simply try harder. If I am trying to control a business, a project, or a relationship and it is failing, then I doggedly do more of what is not working.

If we could agree that for six months we would not ask How?, something in our lives, our institutions, and our culture might shift for the better. It would force us to engage in conversations about why we do what we do, as individuals and as institutions. It would create the space for longer discussions about purpose, about what is worth doing. It would refocus our attention on deciding what is the right question, rather than what is the right answer.

It would also force us to act as if we already knew how—we just have to figure out what is worth doing. It would give priority to aim over speed. At some point we would either find the right question or grow weary of its pursuit, and we would be pulled into meaningful action, despite our uncertainty and our caution about being wrong. It would support us in acting now, rather than waiting until the timing was right, and the world was ready for us. We might put aside our wish for safety and instead view our life as a purpose-filled experiment whose intention is more for learning than for achieving and more for relationship than for power, speed, or efficiency.

> This might elevate the state of not knowing to being an acceptable condition of our existence rather than a problem to be solved, and we might realize that real service and contribution come more from the choice of a worthy destination than from limiting ourselves to engaging in what we know will work.

4 The How? of Why

This book is a discussion of what it takes to live a life in pursuit of what matters. It is an effort to ensure that what we are effective and good at doing is worth doing. The book also raises the question What are we waiting for? By this time we have all been immersed in visioning, guided imagination, and becoming the possibility. We have been mentored and coached and been a mentor and coach to others. So, if we are waiting for more knowledge, more skills, more support from the world around us, we are waiting too long.

In the face of the struggle to know what matters to us, and to act on it, we have to be gentle with ourselves. We live in a culture that lavishes all of its rewards on what works, a culture that seems to value what works more than it values what matters. I am using the phrase "what works" to capture our love of practicality and our attraction to what is concrete and measurable. The phrase "what matters" is shorthand for our capacity to dream, to reclaim our freedom, to be idealistic, and to give our lives to those things which are vague, hard to measure, and invisible. Now, you might say that what actually matters most to you are those things that are measurable, concrete, and do in fact "work." I would not argue with you, but would urge you to explore how focusing too quickly and exclusively on what works can have the effect of distracting us from our deeper purpose and sense of fully living the life we have in mind. In other words, my wish is that we exchange what we know how to do for what means most to us.

How? The Statement

In any of its hundreds of variations when we ask How? we are really making a statement: What we lack is the right tool. The right methodology. We are mechanics who cannot find the right wrench. The question How? not only expresses doubt about whether we know enough and are enough; it also affirms the belief that what *works* is the defining question, a major source of our identity.

The question declares that we, as a culture, and I, as a human being, are fundamentally about getting things done.

If something has no utility, if it does not work, then we consider that a limitation. In fact, talk, dreams, reflections, feelings, and other aspects of who we are as humans are considered lost production in many organizations.

Now, this is not really an argument against the question How? Rather it is an argument that there are more important questions, and How? should be asked later rather than sooner. We are at times so eager to get practical right away that we set limits on ourselves. We become imprisoned in our belief that we don't know how and therefore need to keep asking the question. Also, in our search for tools, we become what we seek: a tool. We reduce ourselves to being primarily pragmatic and utilitarian.

How Many Answers Do We Need?

What is really interesting about How? is that we are asking a question to which we already have the answer. In fact, we have a large group of answers because we have been asking How? for a long time. We have been collecting answers for years, and yet we still keep asking the question.

We are on a treadmill, because although we keep asking How?, we have to wonder what to do with the answers we are getting. No matter how many answers we get, we often decide not to act on them, and when we do act on an answer, what have we got? The fault is in the nature of the question.

Each time we try to act on an answer to the question How?, we will fail because, first, the question wasn't the right question, and second, the answer comes out of someone else's experience, not our own. It is difficult to live another's answer, regardless of the amount of goodwill with which it is offered.

Control in the Balance

One way of understanding the meaning of the question How? is to consider it as an expression of our wish for control and predictability. This is the appeal of the question. We think that we can find control and predictability in the mastery, the knowing, and the certainty of doing something the right way. Not our way, not one way, but the right way. We think there is a right way, that someone else knows what it is, and that it is our job to figure it out. And the world conspires with this illusion, for it wants to sell us an answer. We ask "How?" and the world answers, "This way."

While there are many positive values to our desire for concrete action and results, it does not ensure that what we are doing serves our own larger purpose or acts to create a world that we can believe in—in other words, a world that matters. Thus, the pursuit of How? can act to avoid more important questions, such as whether what we are doing is important to *us*, as opposed to being important to *them*. While we do create value when we pursue what is important to others, it is different from doing what is important to us.

If knowing How? offers us the possibility of more control and predictability, then we may have to sacrifice them to pursue what matters. The choice to worry about why we are doing something more than how we do something is risky business. It is risky for us as individuals, for our organizations, and for society.

Choosing to act on "what matters" is the choice to live a passionate existence, which is anything but controlled and predictable.

Acting on what matters is, ultimately, a political stance, one whereby we declare we are accountable for the world around us and are willing to pursue what we define as important, independent of whether it is in demand, or has market value.

Giving priority to what matters is the path of risk and adventure, but I also believe that the institutions and culture that surround us are waiting for us to transform them into a fuller expression of our own desires. We have the potential to reclaim and experience our freedom and put our helplessness behind us. We have the capacity to experience an intimate connection with other people and with all we come in contact with, rather than feeling that we exist in relationships born of barter and instrumentality. We also have the capacity and maturity to live a life of service and engagement, rather than the primary pursuit of entitlement and interests that focus on ourselves.

But this is getting ahead of the story. I want to begin with a discussion of the wider implications of attending so doggedly to what works and how to do things. What is at stake is not only the quality of our own experience, but also the quality of our institutions and our communities. The primary concern here is the world that we create collectively, for when we commit to bringing our deepest selves to the table, we are transformed by the act of creating something together that we cannot create alone. Therefore any discussion of acting on what matters has to include a discussion of our organizations and our communities. It is in these settings where we will find out who we are. If we can create alternative ways of being when we are organized for a purpose, this will impact the way we manage ourselves in all other aspects of our lives.

What Does Matter

The intent of this book is not to try to convince you about the substance of what matters. It is primarily a discussion of what is required of us if we are to act on what we care about. It helps to differentiate between our beliefs about what makes for effective people and organizations, and the way we approach the realization of those beliefs. This book is about the means of acting on our beliefs. It is about how to realize whatever model of effective organizations we hold to be true.

Each of us has developed a model of what will make for a better world, or at least a better organization. Here are some examples:

1. **Vision, clear purpose, and common goals are essential.** We live into the future that we imagine, and the task is to keep focused on that vision and let that be the context for all our actions.

2. **We need effective tools and problem-solving skills.** When we have the tools, we have the capacity to bring our intentions into being.

3. **Participation and empowerment are key.** So are high involvement and high collaboration. Workers will perform best when they have influence over their workplace and act as owners.

4. **We need flexible structures and sophisticated information systems to support work processes that fit the task and mission.** More agile, cross-functional structures plus easy access to the right information at the right moment create the capacity to meet shifting demands quickly.

5. **Leadership is the key.** We need intuitive, service-oriented, visionary leaders to set the tone and provide the example for those they lead. They must be role models for the change they want to see.

6. **Effective personal skills, good work habits, and behavior that is self-motivating as well as supportive of others are needed.** Behavioral skills and relevant competencies make the difference.

7. **We need learning organizations, places where people are supported to fail, to question their mental models, to experiment with new ways.**

8. **Organizations are places to live out our spiritual and human values.** We need to bring our whole selves to work, where we create an ethical environment that values people as much as results.

These models have all been popular in recent years. What is interesting is that they are all true. Period. Each is a valid expression of what makes for more effective workplaces and lives. They are all important, and we can cite examples where each of these stances has made a difference. So they are in this way all valid statements about what we want to change in the world, at least in the realm of organizational life. Even though the approaches are quite different, there is no point arguing about the value of one over another. If we want to debate which approach is better, then we are just looking to control what happens, we are not looking for insight. In this way, the differences among them do not really matter. Most any path will do.

What does matter is the way that we pursue any of these models. How we act to bring these models into the world takes us to a deeper level, which is a matter of our individual values. Each of us is drawn to a particular set of values that grow out of who we are. Living our values in the pursuit of our preferred organizational model is what matters most. If asked directly, each person resonates to a set of values in a unique way. Consider the words:

Love	Collaboration
Freedom	Justice
Compassion	Reconciliation
Faith in a Supreme Being	Creativity
Integrity	Care for the Next Generation
Equality	

Values such as these are a deeper statement of what really matters to us. They are also what most profoundly connect us to one another and to the world we have created. They come from our own experience with life, especially our woundedness. In a sense,

I desire to create a world that will solve for others what I have struggled with so much for myself.

I would not write so much about freedom if I had not personally felt so constrained. What is interesting about values is that they are all true and noble. There is nothing to argue about here. I have never heard a human value that I didn't like. As with the models of organizational effectiveness, when people argue about "values" it is a guise for seeking control, for imposing their beliefs upon others.

The View from Where We Are

The challenge of values is not to negotiate the importance of one over another, but to act on them. The quality of feeling alive comes when we act on our values, and find a way to bring our own model or strategy for better organizations and communities into the world.

What I want to explore is what is required from us in order to do this. This book weaves together several parallel lines of thought. It is a mixture of ideas about what we are up against and what is required of us to act on our values. At times we have oversold the models and the values, and undersold the difficulty of getting there. I want explore why it is so hard to embody or bring into being what we know to be true. Here is a brief outline of the way this discussion unfolds.

Part **1** *the question*

The first three chapters are about the importance of getting the question right. A major obstacle to acting on what matters is asking questions of methodology too quickly. I have symbolized this by obsessively focusing on the question How? It's not that our pragmatic How? questions are not valid. It's just that when they define the debate we are deflected from considering our deeper values—plus asking How? is a favorite defense against taking action. The pursuit of meaning has been written about a great deal, and sometimes we think that knowing what matters is enough. That our dreams will come true if we just continue to hold them. It is not always so. What we may require is a profoundly different way of seeing and acting on the possibilities. Getting the question right is the first step.

Part **2** *three qualities*

Chapters 4, 5, and 6 explore three aspects of the human condition that support our pursuit of what matters: idealism, intimacy, and depth. These qualities are portrayed as preconditions for acting on our values, intentions, desires. They represent a shift in our mindset, they are the groundwork from which we rise to action. They are some of the hard work, exercise, and diet that are required to live with the risks of pursuing what matters most to us. The underlying themes here are the power of the culture and the choice to reclaim our idealism in a materialistic environment, to reestablish an intimacy with what surrounds us, and to find depth in a world that is happy with a quick makeover.

Part **3** *the requirements*

Our culture is not organized to support idealistic, intimate, and deeper desires. It is organized to reinforce instrumental behavior. If we can understand the nature of the culture, we gain some choice over it. Part 3 takes the discussion of acting on what matters into the workplace. It expands the discussion from what matters to us as individuals to more collective concerns. It shifts our focus from what matters to me to what matters to us.

Part **4** *social architecture*

These final chapters dive deeper into what we are up against when we want to act on what matters in the collective and institutional arena. Part 4 begins with an in-depth exploration of the instrumentality of the culture, and the archetypes of engineer, economist, artist, and architect. The engineer and economist represent mindsets that dominate the culture. The mindset of the artist is increasingly absent in our workplaces. The mindset and role of the social architect is a way of integrating the gifts of the engineer, the economist, and the artist. The idea here is not to completely define the role or work of the social architect. Rather, social architecture is an image, a role for each of us to help create, for acting on what matters in concert with those around us.

the question

We begin with the costs of asking How? too quickly or too eagerly. When we ask how to <u>do</u> something, it expresses our bias for what is practical, concrete, and immediately useful, often at the expense of our values and idealism. It assumes we don't know, and this in itself becomes a defense against action. This section underlines the importance of getting the question right and paying careful attention to the nature of the debate.

Getting the question right may be the most important thing we can do. We define our dialogue and, in a sense, our future through the questions we choose to address. Asking the wrong question puts us in the philosopher's dilemma: We become the blind man looking in a dark room for a black cat that is not there.

how

how is the wrong question.   How? is not just one question, but a series of questions, a family of questions. It is the predominance of this family of questions that creates the context for much of what we do.

How? is most urgent whenever we look for a change, whenever we pursue a dream, a vision, or determine that the future needs to be different from the past. By invoking a How? question, we define the debate about the changes we have in mind and thereby create a set of boundaries on how we approach the task. This, in turn, influences how we approach the future and determines the kind of institutions we create and inhabit. I want to first identify six questions that are always reasonable, but when asked too soon and taken too literally may actually postpone the future and keep us encased in our present way of thinking.

Question One:
How do you do it?

This is the How? question in basic black, serviceable in most situations. It seems innocent enough, and in fact it *is* innocent, for when I ask this question, I take the position that others know, I don't. I am the student, they are the teacher. The question carries the belief that what I want is right around the corner; all that prevents me from turning that corner is that I lack information or some methodology. What this question ignores is that most of the important questions we face are paradoxical in nature. A paradox is a question that has many right answers, and many of the answers seem to conflict with each other. For example, "How do we hold people accountable?" Well, real accountability must be chosen. But if we wait for people to choose accountability, and they refuse, don't we then need to hold them accountable? If we set up oversight systems to ensure this, then what are we getting: accountability or compliance?

The paradoxical questions that lead us to what matters most are those familiar, persistent, complicated questions about our lives, individually and organizationally, that defy clear solutions. We all want to know what we were placed on this earth for, what path is best for us, how to sustain long-term intimate relationships, how to raise a child, how to create a community. At work we try to change the culture, increase performance, find and keep great people, deal with failure, develop leaders, predict where our business is going, be socially responsible. These are large questions, but the small ones also are difficult: Where do I spend this day? Where has the time gone? What is this meeting really about? Why is this project on life support? Where can I get eat a healthy meal? Why don't I get home by 6:00 PM?

We can pursue methods and techniques for answering these questions, or we can appreciate their profound complexity. We can acknowledge the possibility that if there were a methodological answer, we would have found it by now. We can accept the possibility that dialogue and struggle with the question carries the promise of a deeper resolution. Maybe if we really understood what the question entailed, if we approached it as a philosopher instead of an engineer, this would take us to the change or learning that we seek.

The real risk in the "how to do it" question is coming to it too quickly. It finesses deeper questions of purpose, it implies that every question has an answer, and rushes past whether or not we have the right initial question. The rush to a How? answer runs the risk of skipping the profound question: Is this worth doing? And it skirts the equally tough corollary questions: Is this something I want to do? Is this a question that is mine, that matters to me? Or is it a question, or debate, that has been defined by others? And if it has been defined by others, do I have a right to say no to the demand? Here is one more question that precedes methodology: Why are we still asking this question?

You might say that this more profound line of inquiry takes too long, that it can paralyze us from taking decisive action. Well, hold this concern for the moment, because it is just this concern that keeps us operating within boundaries that do not serve us well.

Question Two:
How long will it take?

We live in a culture of speed, short cycle time, instant gratification, fast food, and quick action. So the question of How long? becomes important. Why wouldn't we want everything right now? How long?—like the others—makes its own statement: If it takes too long, the answer is probably no. It implies that change or improvement needs to happen quickly, the faster the better. In this way,

the question How long? drives us to actions that oversimplify the world.

If we believe that faster is better, we choose those strategies that can be acted upon quickly. As individuals, we would rather lose weight with a quick fix of diet pills than the slower, more demanding process of changing a lifetime of eating and exercise habits.

Similarly, in the workplace we choose change strategies that we can act on now. We want changes to occur in days, weeks, and months, not years. This is one appeal of attempting to change the culture by changing the structure, revamping rewards, and instituting short, universal behavior-specific training programs. These are concrete and decision-able actions, amenable to instant execution. Change through dialogue and widespread participation is rejected.

The most important effect of the How long? question is that it drives us to answers that meet the criteria of speed. It runs the risk of precluding slower, more powerful strategies that are more in line with what we know about learning and development. We treat urgency like a performance-enhancing drug, as if calling for speed will hasten change, despite the evidence that authentic transformation requires more time than we ever imagined.

Question Three:
How much does it cost?

The question of cost is first cousin to the question of time. Instead of instant gratification, we seek cheap grace. The question makes the statement that if the price is high, this will be a problem. It embodies the belief that we can meet our objectives, have the life and institutions that we want, and get them all at a discount. It carries the message that we always want to do it for less, no matter how rich we are. For many issues, this is fine. When we are dealing with tangible goods and services, then cost should drive the discussion.

The cost question, however, also controls the discussion of questions that are less amenable to economic determination. At work, there are concerns about safety, about the environment, about the treatment of people; these are larger and vastly more complex issues than getting a product out the door. When we put cost at the forefront, we are monetizing a set of values, and we do this at great risk. At a regional meeting of the National Forest Service I attended, one subgroup felt that services and activities offered by the NFS, such as outdoor education and recreation, as well as commercial use, should be individually costed so as to create a valid marketplace for decisions on how much financial support was needed for each. At stake, though, were the more difficult questions: Whose forests are they? If people do not have the money to pay, should they not have access to public lands? Plus, what impact would essentially commercializing the forest lands have on the goal of preserving them?

Regardless of our personal stance on an issue, when we zero in on cost too soon we constrain our capacity to act on certain values. We value people, land, safety, and it is never efficient or inexpensive to act on our values. There is no such thing as cheap grace. When we consider cost too early or make it the overriding concern, we dictate how our values will be acted upon because the high-cost choices are eliminated before we start.

As individuals, we affect our families and the community we live in by how we address the cost question. We vote on the culture we want by the way we opt to control costs. When we save money at the superstores, we make it difficult for local businesses to survive. When we vote for reduced taxes, we put an unbearable strain on local education and government services.

The question "how much will it cost?" puts the economist at the head of the table. We want the economists to sit with us, but how much do we want them to dominate the discussion? When the cost question comes too early, we risk sacrificing what matters most to us for the sake of economy.

The most common rationalization for doing things we do not believe in is that what we really desire either takes too long or costs too much.

Question Four:
How do you get those people to change?

This is the power question. There are many ways to position it:

"Those people" need to change for the good of the organization, they need to change for their own good, for the good of the family, for the sake of the next generation, for the sake of society. Here are some examples of the ways we hinge our desired future onto someone else's transformation:

- **At Home:** How do you get children to clean up, study more, show respect . . . you name it. How do you get your him or her to pay attention, get a job, show love, stay home . . .

- **At Work:** How do you get top management to walk its talk, work together, be role models, send one message, know we are here . . . you name it.

- **Abroad:** How do you get another culture to work as hard as Americans do, to consume more, save more, live the values of the U.S. corporation . . . in essence, to be more like us.

We may say we want others to change for good reasons. But no matter how we pose the question, it is always a wish to control others. In asking the question we position ourselves as knowing what is best for others.

In all the years I have been doing consulting work and running educational workshops, this is the most common opening question. The majority of all consulting engagements are commissioned with the goal of changing other people's behavior. You constantly hear clients ask, "How do we get those people on board?"—as if we are in the boat and they are not. We want to enroll people, align people, bring them up to speed, motivate them, turn them around, and in the end, get rid of the dead wood.

The desire to get others to change is alive and well in our personal lives also. If only the other person would learn, grow, be more flexible, express more feeling or less feeling, carry more of the load, or be more vulnerable, then our relationship would improve. Most of us enter therapy complaining about the behavior of parents, partners, co-workers, children. While we may package our complaint as a desire to help them, we are really expressing our desire to control them.

The behavior we describe in others may be an accurate description, but that is not the point. The point is, our focus on "those people" is a defense against our own responsibility. The question "How do you get those people to change?" distracts us from choosing who we want to become and exercising accountability for creating our environment. We cannot change others, we can just learn about ourselves. Even when we are responsible for employees or children, we surrender our freedom and our capacity to construct the world we inhabit when we focus on *their* change.

No one is going to change as a result of our desires. In fact, they will resist our efforts to change them simply due to the coercive aspect of the interaction. People resist coercion much more strenuously than they resist change. Each of us has a free will at our core, so like it or not, others will choose to change more readily from the example set by our own transformation than by any demand we make of them. To move away from the spirit of coercion, we replace the question "How do you get them to change?" with "What is the transformation in me that is required?" Or, "What courage is required of me right now?" When we shift the focus to our own actions, we also have to be careful not to ask it as a How? question. This is not a question about methodology, it is a question of will and intention. And when we honestly ask ourselves about our role in the creation of a situation that frustrates us, and set aside asking about their role, then the world changes around us.

Question Five:
How do we measure it?

This question makes the statement "If you cannot measure it, it does not exist." Or to paraphrase Descartes, "I can measure it, therefore it is." So much for love. The engineer in us needs a test to affirm knowledge, a ruler to mark distance, a clock to demonstrate time. We justly want to know how to measure the world. We want to know how we are doing. We need to know where we stand. But the question of measurement ceases to serve us when we think that measurement is so essential to being that we only undertake ventures that can be measured.

Many of the things that matter the most defy measurement. When we enter the realm of human nature and human actions, we are on shaky ground when we require measurable results as a condition of action. As with the questions of time and cost, it is the importance we give the question of measurement that can limit what is placed on the table. A glaring example is student assessment in public education. There are many children whose capacities or accomplishments cannot be measured by a standardized test. We know this, and some schools are developing portfolio alternatives, but our educational system is increasingly driven by a high-stakes testing mentality. When the test becomes the point, then teaching methods and curricula are herded into performing well on the tests. Nontest-related learning becomes secondary.

Our obsession with measurement is really an expression of our doubt. It is most urgent when we have lost faith in something. Doubt is fine, but no amount of measurement will assuage it. Doubt, or lack of faith, as in religion, is not easily reconciled, even by miracles, let alone by gathering measurable evidence on outcomes.

There is also the issue of what use will be made of the measurement. Is it intended for control and oversight, or is it for learning? Is it for the sake of a third party, or for the players involved? The useful aspect of measurement is that it helps us make explicit our intentions. The dialogue about measurement is most helpful when we apply it to ourselves. We need simply to make the subtle shift from "How do you measure this?" to the question "What measurement would have meaning to me?" This opens the discussion on the meaning of the activity and the use of the measures we take. It keeps measurement from being a supervisory device, and turns it into a strategy to support learning.

Measurement is also tricky because we think that the act of measurement itself is a motivational device, and that people will not act on what is not institutionally valued through measurement. This shrinks human motivation into a cause-and-effect dynamic. It implies that if we do not have a satisfactory answer to the measurement question, then nothing will get done. Again, this restricts what we do and pushes us into a world where we only undertake what is predictable and controllable. So much for imagination and creativity.

Question Six:
How have other people done it successfully?

"Where else has this worked?" is a reasonable question, within limits. It is dangerous when it becomes an unspoken statement: If this has not worked well elsewhere, perhaps we should not do it. The wish to attempt only what has been proven creates a life of imitation. We may declare we want to be leaders, but we want to be leaders without taking the risk of invention. The question "Where else is this working?" leads us down a spiraling trap: If what is being recommended or contemplated is, in fact, working elsewhere, then the next question is whether someone else's experience is relevant to our situation—which, upon closer scrutiny, it is not.

The value of another's experience is to give us hope, not to tell us how or whether to proceed.

If the change we contemplate has anything to do with human beings, even the most successful experiment undertaken elsewhere has to be seriously customized for our situation, every time.

This is not to argue against benchmarking, but to express the limits of what value we can actually find in looking elsewhere for how to proceed. Most attempts to transport human system improvements from one place to another have been profitable for those doing the transporting—the consultants—but rarely fulfilled their promise for the end user. Reengineering was a good example of this. The ideas behind reengineering were golden, but its widespread expansion via hard selling from some high-level early adopters led in most cases (60-75% according to its creators) to disappointment and even dysfunction.

▼

Taken in isolation, and asked in the right context, all How? questions are valid. But when they become the primary questions, the controlling questions, or the defining questions, they create a world where operational attention drives out the human spirit. Therapist Pittman McGehee states that the opposite of love is not hate, but efficiency. This is the essence of the instrumental bias, our bias toward action, control, predictability. While being practical is modern culture's child, it carries a price and we are paying it. The price of practicality is its way of deflecting us from our deeper values.

yes

2

yes is the right question.   The alternative to asking How? is saying Yes—not literally, but as a symbol of our stance towards the possibility of more meaningful change. If the answers to How? have not fed us, then perhaps we ordered the wrong meal. The right questions are about values, purpose, aesthetics, human connection, and deeper philosophical inquiry. To experience the fullness of working and living, we need to be willing to address questions that we know have no answer. When we ask How? we limit ourselves to questions for which there is likely to be an answer, and this has major implications for all that we care about.

The goal is to balance a life that works with a life that counts. The challenge is to acknowledge that just because something works, it doesn't mean that it matters. A life that matters is captured in the word *yes*. Yes is the answer—if not the antithesis—to How? Yes expresses our willingness to claim our freedom and use it to discover the real meaning of commitment, which is to say Yes to causes that make no clear offer of a return, to say Yes when we do not have the mastery, or the methodology, to know how to get where we want to go. Yes affirms the value of participation, of being a player instead of a spectator to our own experience. Yes affirms the existence of a destination beyond material gain, for organizations as well as individuals.

To commit to the course of acting on what matters, we postpone the How? questions and precede them with others that lead us to more questions that perhaps lead us to more questions. So much for answers. In fact the most useful questions are ones that entail paradox, questions that recognize that every answer creates its own set of problems. Here are some Yes questions that draw us into what matters.

Question One:
What refusal have I been postponing?

A dominant myth in almost every workplace is that if you say no, you will be shot. The only question is whether our reluctance to say no is more an expression of our own caution and doubt or a feature of the culture that we work in.

If we cannot say no, then our yes means nothing.

When we realize, as Jung stated, that all consciousness begins with an act of disobedience, then saying no opens the door to pursuing our own desires. Refusal becomes a realistic option when we realize that saying no is the beginning of a conversation, not the end. We may say no, and the people we work for may say, "You have to do this." That's okay. I can live without getting my way, but I cannot live without believing that I have a right to refuse what makes no sense to me. The inversion of "What refusal have I been postponing?" is "What have I said yes to that I did not really mean?" Even if I meant yes at the time, I may not mean it now—which says that I have a right to change my mind, which is yet another expression of our freedom and acceptance of our humanity. Machines are consistent, people are not—they only try to be.

Accepting the possibility of refusal means that when we finally say yes it is an act of volition. It is the clearest test of whether we are acting on our own instincts, according to what matters to us, or whether we have internalized the direction provided by others. This is not an argument against following the direction provided by others. It is simply a litmus test: Have we freely chosen to follow their direction, or do we do so out of compliance and a fear of refusing? While we may be doing the same thing either way, the context of our action is everything.

Question Two:
What commitment am I willing to make?

This question recognizes that if change is to occur, it will come from my own free choice, not from the investment of the institution or the transformation of others. Every project of consequence or personal calling will require more of us than we originally imagined. Sister Joyce DeShano, an executive of a large health care system, understands calling better than anyone I know. She says that the call comes from a place that we do not know, that the demands placed on us will be more than we ever expected, and that if we knew what was in store, we never would have said yes. These are excellent tests for the pursuit of what matters.

The question of commitment declares that the essential investment needed is personal commitment, not money, not the agreement of others, not the alignment of converging forces supportive of a favorable outcome. For anything that matters, the timing is never quite right, the resources are always a little short, and the people who affect the outcome are always ambivalent. These conditions offer proof that if we say yes, it was our own doing and it was important to us. What a gift.

Question Three:
What is the price I am willing to pay?

There is a cost to pursuing what matters, and money is the least of it. In acting on what matters, we are leaning against the culture, and we may be disappointing those around us who have adapted to the way we used to be. We may begin a project with little management support. We may initiate discussions that no one else wants to have. We may push our institution into caring about the environment, about its community, about a new service, about new ways of managing performance. All of these carry a risk, and well they should.

Despite its rhetoric, the culture does not value independent action. The culture wants to ask the family of How? questions: What does it cost? How long does it take? Where else has this worked? And we may have no good answers to these questions. When we say Yes instead, we acknowledge that acting on what we choose costs us something, which is what gives it value. If there were no price to saying Yes, to acting in the face of our doubts and meager methodology, then the choice we make would have no meaning.

Asking what price we are willing to pay also means that if we fail, we expect there to be negative consequences. This is one aspect of accountability: If it does not work out, we will not be rewarded. And why should we be rewarded? Because we tried hard? Not really. The fact that being wrong may be costly also means that if we are successful, we will have purchased some latitude to try again, perhaps recapturing some more freedom to act and room to breathe.

Question Four:
What is my contribution to the problem I am concerned with?

This question is an antidote to our helplessness. It affirms that we have had a role in creating the world we live in. If we believe that we have not created what we are facing then the payoff is a moment of guilt-free innocence—it is not our fault. If we decide to choose freedom, we surrender innocence and exchange it for guilt. We experience the guilt of saying no to an individual or an institution, and saying yes to what matters. We gain a life lived well and lose the comfortable innocence of a life partially lived.

This question also shifts the nature of accountability. It is the alternative to being "held" accountable, because it asks us to choose accountability. When we get stuck, and are not acting on what matters, it is usually because we have defined ourselves out of the problem. What keeps us stuck is the belief that someone or something else needs to change before we can move forward. Acknowledging what we have done to cause the problem dislodges us from being trapped in an instrumental existence. This question also gets us out of the audience and onto the stage. We affirm that we are not a spectator, but a player, and in the end we have no one to blame but ourselves. How is that for a strong selling point?

Question Five:
What is the crossroad at which I find myself at this point in my life/work?

This question affirms the idea that it is the challenge and complexity of life and work that gives it meaning. We expected to live happily ever after and find that yesterday's triumph is no longer enough. There is no level of success from which we can wade into shore. This question is especially important if what we have done in the past has been successful, for what worked yesterday becomes the gilded cage of today. It is the answer to this question that gives us clues to what matters most.

The fact that we acknowledge we are at a crossroad gives us the energy to get through the intersection. We will find meaning in exploring and understanding this crossroad. Our crossroad represents an as yet unfulfilled desire to change our focus, our purpose, what we want to pursue. Talking about our crossroad also recognizes that what is most personal to us is also universal. It is always surprising and reassuring to find out that we are not alone and our own crossroad is widely shared by others.

Question Six:
What do we want to create together?

This question recognizes that we live in an interdependent world, that we create nothing alone. We may think we invented something, or achieved something on our own, but this belief blinds us to all that came before and those who have supported us. It is a radical question, for it stabs at the heart of individualism, a cornerstone of our culture. It also declares that we will have to create or customize whatever we learn or whatever we import from others. We may think we can install here what worked there, but in living systems, this is never the case.

Just having a conversation about this question brings people's deeper side into the room. As soon as I begin to discuss what I want to create, I am in the position of cause, not effect. So many workplace conversations are about how we are going to deal with what *they* want to create. Question Six stops the political discussion of what *they* want from us and how we are going to respond, and starts the purpose-filled discussion of what *we* will initiate. The dialogue alone levels the playing field, even if for only a moment. For that moment, our desires count.

The Bonus Question:
What is the question that, if you had the answer, would set you free?

This is the mother of all questions. It is a question that can only be meditated upon. Each time you answer it, you begin a different conversation. While there may not be one answer that you can settle on, each attempt aims you in a good direction. It is like a laser beam into what matters. It brings the question of our freedom front and center. It carries within it the optimistic message that our freedom might be within reach. It confronts our illusions about what will set us free because the answer is a reminder of all the effort it takes that does not set us free, but further obligates us. This question is the culmination of the previous six questions.

All together, the Yes questions transform our inquiries into a deeper, more intimate discussion of why we do what we do. They bring us to the larger question, a favorite of large-scale change consultant Kathie Dannemiller: How will the world be different tomorrow as a result of what we do today? This kind of question brings our purpose into focus. It makes us choose what matters for ourselves. If we want to create a workplace that values idealism, human connection, and real, in-depth learning, we have to create this ourselves. We take a step toward these ideals when we shift to the Yes-type questions, questions that are filled with anxiety and ambiguity, questions that force us to put ourselves on the line.

Towards a More Perfect Union

We can now bring these two sets of questions together, and in so doing, better define the meaning of a shift from How? to Yes—or from "What works?" to "What matters?" Each of the six Yes questions offers an alternative path to the six How? questions. Read the pairs of questions and notice how the locus of control shifts from outside to inside, from practice to intentions, from the strategic to the personal. It might not seem like much, but it is a small shift with large implications.

How? Question One: **How do you do it?**

becomes

Yes Question One: **What refusal have I been postponing?**

The shift here is from a question of method to one of choice. Granted, refusal is a strange way of saying yes. But when our plate is full and we seek a change, knowing what we need to say no to is essential to invention. Many acts of creativity, even new businesses, began with a decision about what not to recreate. The second wave of computer companies were begun by IBM graduates who were determined to create something different.

Also, remember that the question of "How do you do it?" is more often an indirect expression of our doubts than real curiosity. So let the doubts be stated directly and let them be owned by the doubter as an internal struggle in their thinking rather than a detached observation of the external world. Plus, if you believe that saying no will get you shot, well, what a fine way to go.

How? Question Two: **How long will it take?**

becomes

Yes Question Two: **What commitment am I willing to make?**

We have time for all that is truly important to us, so the question of time shifts to What is important? When we say something takes too long, it just means that it does not matter to us. So be it. Don't do it. Schedule is a much later discussion—besides, our ability to know how long a change in a living system will take is a guess at best. How long does it take to raise a child, change a culture, create a new direction, shift a strategy? We can shout urgency, set tight schedules, define monster goals, and the world will still proceed at the pace it chooses. We are too prone to understate the time required as a means of convincing ourselves or others to go ahead. Change comes from care and commitment, so let that be the more important discussion.

How? Question Three: **How much does it cost?**
becomes
Yes Question Three: **What is the price I am willing to pay?**

The real cost of change or creating something of value is emotional, not economic. What is most valuable cannot be purchased at a discount. The price of change is measured by our effort, our will and courage, our persistence in the face of difficulty. The shift here is from an economic measure of cost to a personal measure of will. The price I am willing to pay recognizes this. When we do talk about money, or a budget, it is usually other people's money we will be spending. If it is their money, the stakes are not so high. If we want to raise the stakes so the decision is of some consequence, better to make it a personal question. The ultimate price is the willingness to fail and get hurt if it does not work. This is the more important discussion and leads to a more realistic consideration of whether or not the price is too high.

How? Question Four: **How do you get those people to change?**
becomes
Yes Question Four: **What is my contribution to the problem I am concerned with?**

This is a shift in accountability. The focus on my contribution keeps the decision maker in the loop of accountability. Too many decisions to initiate a change are made by people untouched by the change effort. The Yes question embodies Gandhi's idea that we need to become the change we want to see. This keeps us honest.

It is the antidote to our need to control others. The Yes question affirms that we are the cause, while the How? question declares they are the cause. Better we than they. Gandhi had another precept that I once saw on the wall of his ashram: "If blood be spilled, let it be our own." This defines humility and a willingness to sacrifice, and our thinking about change needs more of this.

How? Question Five: **How do we measure it?**
becomes
Yes Question Five: **What is the crossroad at which I find myself at this point in my life/work?**

The central question in exploring a change is whether or not what we are considering will have meaning for us, for the institution, for the world. Concrete measures can determine progress, but they do not really measure values. The crossroad question helps to define what has personal meaning for us, which is the first-order question. We pursue what matters independently of how well we can measure it, so by looking at the crossroad we break the limitations demanded by the measurement question. It is important to measure what we can, but to raise this question too early, and to use it as a criterion that will determine whether or not to proceed, runs the risk of worshipping too small a god.

How? Question Six: **How are other people doing it successfully?**
becomes
Yes Question Six: **What do we want to create together?**

These questions represent the tension between what is proven and what is still to be discovered. If we want our institution to hold a leadership position, then we need a question that does not distract us too much by holding too closely to the experience of others. Individually and collectively, we have the wisdom we need to get the results we want. The challenge is to trust and act on that wisdom. How many times have we brought in an outsider to tell us what we already knew was true?

"Where else is it working?" has a compelling face validity. Who would argue against learning from others? The problem is that the question perpetuates the belief that others know and we don't. The Yes question shifts towards the knowledge of those who have a stake in the change and affirms our trust in ourselves. Remember the childhood game of hide and seek? The search began when the one who was "it" called out, "Ready or not, here I come!" A profound statement.

The Paradox of How?

We can now thread these concerns together. Whatever our destination, it is letting go of the practical imperative that is most likely to guide us to a larger sense of where we want to go and what values we want to embody in getting there. What matters is the experience of being a human being and all that this entails.

What will matter most to us, upon deeper reflection, is the quality of experience we create in the world, not the quantity of results.

There is no methodology for recovering our idealism. Why follow in the steps of another to discover where our dreams will lead us? If we believe there is only one recipe for this discovery, the method we have ingested will contaminate our own answer to the question of purpose.

The array of Yes questions brings meaning and reminds us that if freedom is what is essential to a life that matters, and to an institution that fulfills its purpose, then along this path are acts of disobedience and even betrayal—a willingness to move against the dominant beliefs of the moment. I am always surprised at how willing people in power are to follow the current fashion. The moment one high-profile institution, in concert with a big-name consulting firm, reengineers, empowers, merges, divests, flattens, kisses customers, or emphasizes cost control, the chain reaction of follow-the-leader is immediate and widespread. When we follow fashion and ask for steps, recipes, and certainty, we deny our freedom, for we are trapped by the very act of asking the question. Following a recipe assumes there is a known path to finding our freedom and that someone else knows it. Freedom asks us to invent our own steps. The phrase that expresses this most clearly is "to be the author of our own experience."

This does not mean that we cannot learn from others. It is just that asking how is a poor method of learning. We learn by bearing witness to how others live their lives. We learn from the questions others have the courage to ask. We are more likely to be transformed from dialogue about what is real and what is illusion. These conversations are qualitatively different from seeking methods and answers.

▼

When we look for tools and techniques, which are part of the How? question, we preempt other kinds of learning. In a sense, if we want to know what really works, we must carefully decide which are the right questions for this moment. Picking the right question is the beginning of action on what matters, and this is

what works. This is how we name the
debate, by the questions we pursue, for
all these questions are action steps.
Good questions work on us, we don't
work on them. They are not a project to
be completed but a doorway opening
onto a greater depth of understanding,
action that will take us into being more
fully alive.

3

defense

defenses against acting. Changing the focus from
questions about practicality to questions about personal commitment entails more than simply a shift in agenda or a change in
conversation. When we embrace the Yes questions, we are con-
fronted with our freedom. Most of the messages of our culture
deny our freedom and tell us that we are products of our environment, driven by rewards and self-interest, and that those in
power hold our future in their hands. To truly act on our own
values and pursue what matters means that we need to accept, at
the level of bone marrow, that we are free and therefore responsible for the actions we choose, regardless of our environment
and its messages.

The most difficult aspect of acting on what matters is to come face
to face with our own humanity—our caution, our capacity to
rationalize our willingness to fit into the culture rather than live
on its margin. This is true in our neighborhood, among col-
leagues, and in the workplace. Fundamentally, to act fully on
what matters means we are asked to claim our freedom and live
with the consequences. The subtlety with which we deny our
freedom warrants a lifetime of exploration, but what follows are
some examples that are germane to this discussion.

The Boss Is Cause

The first line of defense against freedom is to pay attention to
people in power. Many of the How? questions carry the statement that the future is in someone else's hands: the politicians,
the media, management, the unions, the government. When we
seek their support and hold them responsible for our institutions,
we reinforce our own helplessness. We do this when we credit
them with our success and blame them for failure. The persistent
"How do we get top management support?" is the embodiment

of the belief that someone else is vital to change, and this is a very popular question.

When you or I suggest that leadership is not that crucial, few people like the message. Most claim that we have not met *their* top management, that we are naïve about the power of the position—the discussion is endless. Some will actually get angry if you persist with the argument that we give the power to and, in this way, create those at the top. Nelson Mandela, the recipient of worldwide admiration, has stated that the moment you treat a man as if he is a god, you have invited the devil into existence.

The devil, in this instance, is not the behavior of the boss or politician; the devil is the denial of our own power and the expectation that someone else will lead us to a better tomorrow.

The belief that the power lies "up there" is a way of ensuring our own helplessness, all for the relief of an imagined moment of safety.

The Will to Analyze and Seek Concrete Data

We also deny ourselves action when we keep looking for more and more information to ensure greater certainty about the future as a condition of moving on. We can turn curiosity into a life stance, in which life is to be studied, measured, submitted to a continual cost-benefit analysis, rather than lived. We can make a career of evaluating the adventures of others. The will to evaluate and measure is in the same category as the will to hold power. The illusion is that if we can conduct enough research on changes in human systems, the results will be persuasive. My experience is that data and measures are not half as persuasive as anecdotes. Anecdotes, personal stories, reminiscences like biblical parables, are the medium through which faith is restored. Stories are a form of poetry, and give us a saving image to personally relate to. The persistent questions about data and evidence are most often a form of disagreement, or despair, or show a lack of faith. There is little discussion of faith in organizations, but it is only with faith that significant changes can begin.

When Is a Cigar Just a Cigar?

When is a How? question useful and not a defense against change? Of course, questions can be a genuine search for more information. They become suspect when no answer will satisfy. I become wary when people ask how, get an answer, and ask how again and again and again. Stand in the presence of any member of the How? family: What are the steps to changing culture? How do you handle difficult people? Where is this working? When the answer is offered and each time the question snaps back like a rubber band, you know that doubt or caution is the real subject of discussion, not methodology or data.

When no answer satisfies, and people continue to act as if they do not understand, then the wrong question is being asked.

Then, the question about How? is not for information, but is a defense against an alternative and unpredictable future.

Authentic questions, on the other hand, are asked with the expectation that those doing the questioning will join in devising an answer. The question is not used to make a statement, or to minimize choice. A question about method has value when we are willing to act on its answer. When a question is followed by a series of additional questions, then beware. Be especially careful of the questions about measurement. We all want evidence, but each of us must consider this: When the measurement question is asked as if someone else, working independently, must prove value, then the question is a refusal in disguise. It is fine to refuse, but say it directly, don't disguise it as a search for data.

The Risks Are Real

I want to acknowledge that to confront people with their free-dom—in this case, to face them with intimate and paradoxical questions and postpone getting into the familiar territory of the pragmatic—is to invite their anger. Many will resent the demand to bring their personal ideals or longings into the dis-cussion. We hear charges that the Yes questions are too per-sonal, as if business were not a personal thing. There is a cul-tural contempt, especially in the media, for anything that smacks of "touchy feely," touching and feeling.

This means that the answer—that you are a free soul, responsi-ble for the future of your institution and your environment—is quite indigestible. That is the problem with this book. Anyone who acts on its message risks being accused of being too abstract, or too philosophical, or naïve and unproven in the "real world," or a fan of New Age spirituality. Someone will note that there are few examples where these ideas have worked, where they can be credited with a major turnaround. The most cynical response to idealism and the pursuit of mean-ing is the claim that most people do not care about meaning. What they want is a better lifestyle. They want higher pay, better benefits, not more responsibility. They want better bosses, not more freedom.

These objections have some validity, but what they likely mean is that the people making them are saying no to the ideas of free-dom, choice, and accountability. I would support them in their refusal. The only response to these concerns is to acknowledge them and encourage those voicing them to just say no. Part of freedom is the right to deny the existence of freedom.

We Make It So

We all, in some way, defend against acting on our values and intentions by denying that we are, in fact, helping to create the culture that pressures us towards safety and a methodological existence. We complain about the culture as if we were only visitors here. We want to hold top management responsible for creating organizational culture, and we each have our favorite culprits to blame for taking the society in a direction that distresses us. As individuals we keep our heads down, believe that there will be time later to act on our intentions, and choose to dismiss the more difficult, ambiguous, and personal questions that deal with the meaning of our work and our experience.

The problem is that when we invest emotionally and economically in—in fact, organize ourselves around—safety, control, and predictability, we postpone the deeper questions of what matters. The cost to ourselves and our institutions is the quality of being alive. In every concert Bruce Springsteen cries out, "Is anybody alive out there?" Interesting question. The pursuit of what matters is about bringing the quality of being alive to everything we do. This is, ultimately, the reward for pursuing our desires.

Escape from Freedom

Part of the appeal of making How? the question of choice is that it lifts the requirement of going deeper and reflecting on our ideals. We say we do not have time for this, but there are deeper reasons to postpone depth, for it can make us anxious. Pursuing How? is the safer path, the more comfortable path. Asking How? thereby is a way to avoid anxiety or, as philosopher Eric Fromm would say, to "escape from freedom."

What we really want is both freedom *and* safety, but they are strange bedfellows. Freedom gets confused with liberty (which means we are not oppressed). Freedom is not doing your own thing, but just the opposite. It means we are the authors of our own experience. It means we are accountable for the well being of all that is around us. It means we believe that we are constituting, or creating, the world in which we live. This belief is rare for most of us, because mostly we feel helpless. At these moments, we wish for better leaders, better government, and someone else to create the conditions for us to be free. As if someone else can give us our freedom.

The dilemma is that we do not want to pay for our freedom. We want to drive fear out of the workplace. We want someone else to assure us of a safer tomorrow. We want to know how: how to do it, how much it costs, how long it will take, how to get those people to align with us, how to measure it, and who else is doing it. All of this is a wish to go to heaven and not have to die. We want certainty before we act. And we want those in power to bless us. We have been willing to yield sovereignty to our bosses or institutions in return for their promise to take care of us. This bargain is disappearing through no action of our own, but the disappearance of safety is hard to live with.

As long as we wish for safety, we will have difficulty pursuing what matters.

Loss of Faith

Asking How? is also a defense against our own loss of faith. It is a defense that the culture strongly rewards. The culture promises security through answers and the bottom line. The question is whether it is a real or illusory promise. Knowing how to do something may give us confidence, but it does not give us our freedom.

Freedom comes from commitment, not accomplishment. It comes from finding our own voice, not following another's. Continually asking how is a form of self-restraint and even subjugation. I am acting at that moment as if I am not quite ready; I need one more lesson to be able to cook, sing, manage, raise a child, hit a tennis ball, motivate others, live to be one hundred and one.

In this way, How? becomes an expression of our lack of trust in ourselves. Instead of choosing the life we want, we postpone it. We believe that we are not enough, that we don't have it together. We think that we must attend one more workshop, read one more book, get a college degree if we don't have one, an advanced degree if we do. We think we must have a recipe if we are hungry, a personal trainer if we are out of shape (who isn't?), plastic surgery if we are looking older, and we go shopping when all else fails.

Shopping is a culturally approved way to assuage our anxiety and postpone going deeper within to the core of our experience. If performing and accomplishing my way out of anxiety fails, maybe I can purchase relief. I was in a high-end lingerie shop in New York once and I asked the salesperson, "Who buys this expensive underwear?" She said that men buy it when they feel guilty and women buy it when they feel depressed—in a consumer culture, we believe that we can spend and shop our way out of anxiety and pain. I forget, now, what I was doing in that store.

The Mask of Confusion

There are times when leaders ask us to make a change and we respond by acting confused. We continue to ask How? when we do not really mean it; the confusion is just a measure of our discontent. We act like we are confused, like we don't understand.

The reality is that we *do* understand—we get it, but we don't like it. At work, when management says we have to shift culture, structure, strategy, we may think they are wrong. Since we think we cannot say that directly, we instead ask them to provide more detail, define roles, give us the tools, the blueprint for what they have in mind. If they respond to our requests, it rarely makes a significant difference. The effect of the effort to eliminate "confusion" is simply to delay the change.

This Is It

Our wish for quick action and our love of tools, useful as they can be, distract us from our own values and the reality of our own experience.

Endlessly seeking more tools, more skills, more methodology deflects us from accepting our humanity, our limitations, the fact that the questions that trouble us are inherent in being human and have no real answers.

We are as together as we are ever going to be and it may not be enough. My body is not in the shape I want it to be; I am getting older and a flat stomach won't change that; the quality of my meal will not satisfy the hunger in my heart; no amount of shopping will cure my loneliness.

To live our lives fully, to work wholeheartedly, to refuse directly what we cannot swallow, to accept the mystery in all matters of meaning—this is the ultimate adventure. The pursuit of certainty and predictability is our caution speaking. Freedom is the prize, safety is the price, what is required is faith more than fact and will more than skill.

The Price of Not Acting on What Matters

This chapter has been about our resistances to acting on what matters. Let me summarize here what has been suggested above:

- First, our resistance isolates us from a deeper intimacy with ourselves, which is the wish to understand, to wonder why, to find our purpose, to let other people in, to express our feelings, and to affirm our humanity.

- Second, it robs from us one aspect of our freedom: the capacity to pursue what matters to us, to create a world that we believe in according to our values, independent of the marketplace or what is fashionable at the moment.

- Third, the decision to ask the How? questions first and postpone the questions of meaning, the Yes questions, has a pervasive effect on how we experience our work as well as the optimism we feel about the organizations we inhabit. It influences the way we think about our lives and the larger society, especially the production/consumption engine that drives it. The love of what is practical and concrete reinforces a culture of materialism. Most of us see clearly the economic materialism out there, but this is simply an expression of the spiritual materialism within us.

▼

The challenge is not that we do not know what matters to us; it is that sustaining our actions becomes unbearably burdensome. At those moments when we have the space to consider what is in our hearts and what dreams remain for us to fulfill, the task can seem monumental and treacherous. Often we become clearer about what matters to us when we are in

a protected learning or spiritual environment: a retreat, a sanctuary, a vacation
conversation, a workshop, or a coaching
experience. In a moment of clear thinking
and feeling about what matters to us, we
may be determined to act on our insight.
But as we return to the mainstream of
daily life, the determination can become
diluted. What happens is that when we
reenter the culture with all of its power,
we face once again the commitments we
have made, and the expectations of
those around us. The pull of getting things
done and the questions of How? exert
their force. These are the moments when
what matters and what works seem most
at odds with each other. What follows
are ideas that help sustain our intentions
in the face of it all.

three qualities

To fully benefit from questions of purpose and commitment, we need to be grounded in certain qualities that help us hold to our personal intentions when we engage with the pressures of the marketplace. These qualities are our capacity for reawakening our <u>idealism</u>, our ability to become more <u>intimate</u> in the way we contact the environment, and our willingness to choose <u>depth</u> in the face of the ever-quickening pace of modern life. The culture has forsaken idealism for cynicism, it has foregone intimacy for consumption and virtual experience. As a result, we find ourselves alienated and isolated, regardless of the crowd that we move in. Finally, in an effort to go fast, we sacrifice depth. When we lose idealism, intimacy, and depth, we function at a cosmetic level, pushed along by fashion, out of touch with our center, and we react as if we are the effect of the culture, rather than its cause.

idealism

recapturing the idealism of youth. We are
to balance our concern with what works with what
What is lost in a materialistic and pragmatic culture is o
ism. Idealism is a state of innocence that has the potential to bring
together our larger purpose with our day-to-day doing. Idealism
is required to reclaim our freedom, for at the end of it all, it is our
freedom that gives us the possibility to more fully live our lives.

In Praise of the Impractical

Idealism is the pursuit of the way we think things should be. Webster's definition of an idealist is "one who follows their ideals, even to the point of impracticality." This takes us right to the place we want to be, the place of practicality in the pursuit of our desires. It confronts us with the question of who decides what is possible and what is practical. Who draws the line, and do we perhaps yield too quickly on what others define as impractical?

There was a time in each of our lives when we were more idealistic than practical. A young child asks for the moon and expects it to be delivered. As we grow older and enter what is called the "real world," our idealism is assaulted. Our idealism is thought of as weakness—a flaw in perception, an unwillingness or, worse, an incapacity to see the world as it really is. To be told you are idealistic and therefore unrealistic is a painful accusation. Idealism is the province of the child, a sign of immaturity. When are you going to grow up and get it?

Too Real, Too Soon

The pressure for realism is introduced at what seems to be an increasingly early age. Perhaps it is the media, or what is happening in the streets, in our communities, or the transient nature of our lifestyle, or the easy electronic exposure to the larger world. But whatever your theory about this might be, our children start adapting to the "real world" at younger and younger ages. We contribute to this realism by urging our children to learn more quickly. As soon as they begin school, we start worrying about their SAT scores and college. We fill their afternoons and weekends with developmental activities. We are happy when they win at sports, for we think this is a leading indicator of their future. Early in the game the child is asked to shift from experiencing life to preparing for it.

The push towards early adulthood undermines the possibility of prolonged idealism. And why not? Idealism is hard to defend, for data and history seem to be on the side of realism and practicality, almost by definition. How can you defend idealism . . . by measuring its value? Idealism dissolves in a world where measurement and instant results are the most acceptable answers. The result is a socially acceptable cynicism. Cynicism is a defense against idealism, and cynicism is so powerful because it has experience on its side. We each have our wounds. We each have our story of idealism unrewarded or even punished. Cynicism is the safe ground, for it is the ultimate defense against disappointment. The effect is that the idealist is discounted, even considered a fool.

I am one of those fools. One of my character flaws is that I am a dreamer. The rap against the books I write and the talks I give and the way I am in the world is that I am not realistic. That I am out of touch with the harsh reality of life. That I view life from a lofty perch, forgetting what it is like in the trenches. All of which is true.

Self-Interest Becomes the Bottom Line

Conventional wisdom makes several arguments against idealism. We have come to accept as true the economist's claim that behavior is basically driven by self-interest. This seems to be affirmed by the entitlement culture that we live in. We organize our institutions around the principle of self-interest, and this gives rise to the question "What's in it for me?" This question traps us in a utilitarian world. The implication is that if you do not come up with a decent offer, I am not interested. I have a right to something more from you, you owe me something, and if I commit myself to an organization, you must give the devil (in this case my self-interest) its due.

"What's in it for me?" declares that for me to care about something larger, there must be a payoff. My commitment is up for barter. If my commitment is conditional on your response, or on your delivery of a promise, then it never really was a commitment. It was a deal.

Real commitment is a choice I make regardless of what is offered in return.

People in power reciprocate the self-centeredness of "What's in it for me?" when they, in turn, ask, "How do we get those people to commit?" Once we have begun this exchange—which is really the commercialization of commitment—we have excluded the possibility of authentic, personal commitment and the willing pursuit of our own desires and ideals. People in power despair over finding commitment without resorting to devices designed to "get" someone to do something. Employees abandon their desires because they think they won't be rewarded.

This creates such a widely accepted barter mentality that any discussion of individual ideals and desires has been relegated to our private lives. We've replaced desire with the discussion of needs: what they are and what we can exchange to satisfy them. John McKnight and Ivan Illich have written extensively about how when we talk of people's needs, we convert people from citizens to consumers. We shrink the human spirit when we define needs, because it has us acting out of our deficiencies rather than from our capacities. And we barter away one of our greatest capacities, which is the capacity to dream and to pursue that dream, simply for its own sake.

It is common to get stuck complaining about the culture of entitlement, how generation XYZ is in it for themselves—and whatever happened to gratitude?—but this a tired conversation. The questions that are most compelling are: What does it mean when we lose contact or faith in our ideals, or our dreams and desires? Why would we give up the pursuit of our desires if the right offer does not come along? Why have I placed my desires up for auction? When did I decide that I could live without them or postpone them until I have implemented my exit strategy?

Idealism is the willingness to pursue our desires past the point of practicality. The surrender of desire is a loss of part of our self. Desire is an affair of the heart. My heart's desire. This is why the word *desire* is so out of place in a world of commerce. Matters of the heart, such as our deepest values, are not open to negotiation. The heart cannot be explained, or reasoned with, or commanded. The heart longs, it suffers and breaks, it desires. The economist has no interest in affairs of the heart because they cannot be predicted or traded; in other words, they cannot be managed. The discounting of desire is a loss of faith that there could be any alternative to the world as defined by the economist.

Barter as a Last Resort

We are willing to barter our commitment when we have no more authentic, or desire-based, commitment to give, because we forget for that moment what we are willing to sacrifice for. In this way barter becomes the booby prize. In the absence of knowing what I can give myself over to, or the willingness to place myself at risk for an unknowable and uncertain outcome, I am willing to come to the table and play Let's Make a Deal with my idealism. Who wouldn't want to be a millionaire at these moments?

To freely choose barter as the basis for work is to commercialize our relationships and ourselves. I treat myself as a transaction in the making. I value myself according to what I can get for myself. My market value becomes my only value. I am now worth what the market will bear. So why wouldn't I get the highest price possible?

Part of the price of becoming a transaction is that we allow our value to be defined by others: an organization, a boss, a recruiter, a partner, a lover. I become a commodity whose worth rises and falls according to the marketplace. I place my self-esteem in the hands of forces that I cannot control. I am happy when the price rises and feel depressed in periods of recession—and I am literally depressed in times of deflation.

The economic model of the person affirms instrumental relationships that are held together by the nature and value of the exchange.

I am willing to do what is rewarded, I want desperately to know what they value, I refuse to do what is not rewarded, and I want greater rewards, especially when I deliver greater and greater results. Ultimately, no level of reward is enough, for my work and my purpose have become a game. Winning more becomes the point, for I need the game to feel valued.

What I may not realize is that when I choose this path, I sacrifice my own purpose. The choice of purpose and the rules of engagement are no longer mine, they belong to the marketplace—and the marketplace knows how to take advantage of that.

Calling and Commitment

There is an alternative to the barter model. It is to believe that people want to contribute to an institution and need not be purchased to do so. Paid yes, but purchased no. There are other sources of motivation besides a negotiated exchange. There are elements of desire that want to be expressed. There are many examples of people choosing work because they simply want to do it, not because of the material rewards. This is, in fact, what some have called the artist's way. It also the teacher's way, many civil servants' way, the way of those who have chosen a religious path.

In the eyes of commerce, a calling is a luxury and the artist is seen as either a fool or a terrorist—they do not live by the rules of commerce or within the bonds of loyalty. They are loyal only to their own art, their own values, their own idealism. They are no more dangerous or rare than those who choose the more instrumental path, they just value their own free, subjective experience enough that they have chosen to not be defined by the economic model.

Virtue Is Its Own Reward

You may ask, Why would someone commit themselves to the success of a business unless the rewards were there? To which I would reply, Well, what happened to virtue? Virtue is advertised to be its own reward. It does not do well, however, when we define the game as the economic pursuit of all that is practical and immediately useful. When we only treasure How? and devalue all questions of "For what purpose?" and "For whose sake?" we send virtue into hiding. And with virtue's retreat, sacrifice, commitment, faith, and her other cousins are left in the cold.

With the loss of inside-out commitment, our institutions also suffer. The possibility that people will voluntarily care for the whole disappears. Instead of seeing that we are part of the cause, we think it is in people's nature to be self-centered and interested in their own small silo. So we then conclude that the only way that care for the whole will exist is if we purchase it. Then the prophecy is complete. Our belief in the barter model proves that money is the only voice that speaks. The fact that we have actively silenced individual desires and authentic commitment never even gets defined as a problem for management.

Besides costing the individual a more compassionate version of themselves, the economic model also costs the community. This is the loss of philanthropy. So rare has altruism become that the word is unfamiliar from lack of usage. Though large organizations give money to the community, acts of philanthropy have become part of a business strategy. For example, the Public Broadcasting System used to ask for funding for its programming by going to the foundation or community relations departments of large corporations. During the 1980s, however, they were told to contact the marketing department for a decision on what to fund. Intentions that began as philanthropy have now converted to marketing and image building.

Freedom for Sale

There are emotional forms of barter that are even more significant than economic transactions.

The barter mindset treats every act as if it were driven by the exchange value for the players.

Everything is offered up for auction, the most precious of which is our own freedom: We are willing to surrender our freedom, especially in the workplace, in return for protection and promotion. We surrender sovereignty to the boss and they in turn protect us and look out for our interests.

This is a bargain that goes back at least to medieval times when the feudal lord offered the protection of a walled city to the peasants in return for dominion over them. He was the lord; they were required to serve him through taxes, sex, and other forms of allegiance. He, in turn, maintained a fighting force and security system for their safety. Straightforward deal. Subjugation in return for safety.

Bring this forward to modern institutions, and employees make a similar bargain. We will follow orders, live with the management style of the boss, defend the interest of the unit in exchange for the boss's advocacy of our interests. A small example: I heard an executive state that he was troubled by managers competing over who got promoted. He was in a personnel planning meeting where all of the division managers fought for the promotion of their own people, with little concern for the well being of the larger institution.

Why would these executives think their own people were better than others and act out of some kind of familial imperative? You might say this is in the nature of being human and there may be some truth in this. But more likely it was the executives attempting to deliver on the patriarchal promise, the bargain of loyalty in exchange for protection and promotion. They have to advocate for their own people to meet their contractual obligations.

It is easy to blame the boss for becoming a baron. I think the choice and mentality of the subordinate are more significant. We offer parts of ourselves, our desires, our freedom, as part of the

bargain and so expect our bosses to fight for our interests every
chance they get. And when they do, we think we have made a
good deal. At this moment we begin to believe that in order to
be successful, we must put our freedom on the table. When we
are rewarded, at least we sold it for a good price.

Naming the Debate

In the barter framework, the cost of the bargain is dependency:
We have become so dependent on our institutions and their
agents that we think they hold the key to what we most dearly
seek. When we think that the only way we can get what we want
is to bargain for it, we hand over power to others, including the
power to define reality.

We yield the capacity to define what matters. We encourage the
institution to define what matters for us by asking our leaders
what is important to them. I listen when they list the five values
that we should operate under. I want to know what their objectives are and how we should achieve them. I let the organization
tell me who I am when I take their feedback seriously. I want my
boss to be my mentor. I work on myself in line with their suggestions; in fact, if I do not get feedback from my boss, I am disappointed. The consequence is that I do not feel I can be myself
and also be successful. At least, not until I get near the end of the
line and can wade into shore.

At Home as Well as Work

Like every other element of our passion for practicality, the
barter belief system also bleeds into our personal relationships. I
think that to get what I want from my partner, someone I love,
I must consciously offer something of value in return. The
destructive element in this is not that there needs to be balance
in the relationship, which there does. It is that I have become

instrumental about what I offer. I have heard myself talk about all that I have "invested" in a relationship. Well, when did a relationship become an investment decision? Did I fall in love with the expectation of a return on that "investment"? Am I a friend as long as I get something back? Or as long as the relationship "works"? Have you ever heard yourself suggest to a family member that we have a "meeting"? I have.

There needs to be a place for the mystery and surrender and forgiveness that characterize idealism, in our work and our personal lives. These conditions are not amenable to barter or exchange. Mystery means that much of what matters may be unspeakable, or unknowable. Surrender, in a spiritual sense, would lose its value if done for effect. Forgiveness is not forgiveness if given with the expectation of return.

Talking in these terms is a way of reestablishing our respect for idealism. It is the artist in each of us speaking. It is believing in something for its own sake, a rediscovery of innocence in the best sense. It entails giving up some of our sophistication and cynicism. This becomes the stuff of what matters. It entails some risk, subjects us to possible scorn, especially from the economists. All of which makes it unsafe and trustworthy. It may be that only when we stop thinking in terms of barter, and market value, are we ready to experience our freedom once again. Not only our freedom to act on our own choices, but our freedom to take our dreams seriously, and return idealism to the place where we once kept it sacred.

▼

The point to focusing on idealism is that it
is part of what can sustain us when we
act on our values. Our idealism gives us

the conviction to bring the models of effective organizations into the world in a way that affirms our deepest values, regardless of whether the world reinforces our efforts. For example, if we say that what we care most about is compassion, justice, and reconciliation, then these qualities will define how we implement the model of the workplace we believe in. Our idealism allows us to act on our values for their own sake and not be lured by more barter-based, self-interested strategies of action. We advocate tactics of living out our commitment and do not expect to be rewarded for following this path. Otherwise, the kind of organization we want to create (our model) gets polluted by the way we try to bring it into being (the means). We get caught up with the ends justifying the means. To avoid this, we recapture our idealism as one of the preconditions to acting on what matters.

5

intimacy

sustaining the touch of intimacy. The second condition for acting on what matters is to choose intimacy in the face of an instrumental world. The challenge is to sustain our humanity when all around us is in the process of being automated. Intimacy is about the quality of contact we make: It values direct experience over electronic or virtual experience. It is immersion into the world of feelings, connection with the senses, and vulnerability—all of which, not incidentally, are considered liabilities in our institutions. In an instrumental world people are considered assets, resources to be leveraged; they are not valued as unique and highly variable human beings. Institutions are based on consistency and predictability, while intimacy relies on variation and surprise.

The Pull of Disconnection

Instrumentality turns our bodies into tools—or, in the end, crops. My friend Peter Koestenbaum tells of conducting a Philosophy in Business seminar with an oil company. As he begins to speak, one of the participants interrupts and says, "We want you to know, professor, that we have brains made of cement."

Peter responds, "Well, you have a heart, don't you?"

"We call that a pump."

In the world of commerce, the heart becomes a pump. Everything gets defined by its utility—so often and for so long—that we apply that thinking to our own selves: My body is no longer valued as the temple of my soul, but as a commodity, a mechanical puzzle, the ultimate clockworks. There will come a time when my body will become completely replaceable, from my brain to my heart, as well as all the rest of my organs and limbs. And if there is a spare parts shortage, no problem, my body can be cloned—an exact copy of myself can be made. Supply and demand. Upon death, my net worth goes up. My organs, when harvested and sold off individually, have a market value of close to a million dollars. So in the end, the sum of my parts could be worth a great deal more than the whole. When this happens the world of commerce has transformed the human body into a product. Quite a contrast to the idea of the body as the physical incarnation of our existence.

> Intimacy is a relationship to the world where feelings, touch, sight, and smell are the point. Close contact with another person, with nature, a work of art, an idea, our own bodies—these are all elements of living intimately.

Intimacy requires free and willing disclosure, often at the expense of instrumental values such as role playing, control, and negotiation. Intimacy values the detail and nuances of life, it cares for the color, shape, and light in a room. It attends to the detail of interaction with other people. It is sensitive beyond comfort and recognizes the pain of existence. Intimacy cares more about the fate of a person than the success of an institution. In this way, intimacy can become a political stance that seems to endanger institutions. This is one reason we fear intimacy in the workplace: If we get too close to an idea, or people, or even a product, we will not have the detachment necessary to engage in tough institutional surgery.

Intimacy, like idealism, has little market value. Intimacy can't really be measured and is difficult to price and purchase, try as we might. When you think of becoming an artist (the archetype of someone who is on intimate terms with nature, with ideas, and with the world of the senses), the word *starving* follows quickly. Intimacy also implies an element of activism, the willingness to show up—often. It is to be in dialogue with others, to be in their presence often enough to know what they look like, think about, feel like. It is the experience of sharing doubts and talking through differences. It is a contact sport, where touch is fundamental.

The Virtual Experience

Intimacy is becoming obsolete with the growth of the electronic culture. We choose video conferences rather than face-to-face meetings, we attend school online, we email, voicemail, and more, all for the sake of cost and efficiency. As Robert Putnam and others keep reminding us, civic engagement and social capital, which are collective forms of intimacy, are on the decline in our communities. We stay home at night, the porch has moved to the back of the house, and we are too busy or too exhausted to join in activist, collective endeavors. We only show up in numbers for sports and entertainment. Instead of contact sports, we want spectator sports.

In its ability to replace or enhance human effort, computer technology also changes the nature of human experience. For all its ability to make the world work better, it may unintentionally increase my feelings of detachment and reduce my capacity to sustain an intimate relationship, not only with people, which is always difficult, but with my environment, my workplace, my neighborhood, my world.

One way to view the impact of technology on our experience is to notice how it drives us towards a more virtual existence. Virtual is defined as "being in effect, though not in actual fact" (Webster). Virtual reality gives us the appearance or simulation of an experience, without having the experience itself. Much of the electronic technology offers us efficiency and infinite access to information, instead of direct experience. The direct experience it does offer is with a monitor, a keyboard, and a variety of magical devices. Where I once knew the bank teller, now I am friends with my ATM machine. Where I once went to a store to shop, I now go online. In all of this I gain convenience, but sacrifice human and material contact.

Intimacy as Marketing Strategy

Language is another example. We are defined by our language and we are increasingly bringing the language of technology into our daily dialogue. What was conversation is now considered "information exchange." When we want a private conversation we "talk offline." When we talk about "community," we are referring to a long-distance network with people we may never have met.

And commerce is now co-opting for its own use the language of relationship. We now hear the term *customer intimacy*. A large technology company proudly advertises that it is "in the relationship-building business" and offers the latest ways to develop customer intimacy. What they mean by "relationship building" is knowing enough about me to have the right product at the right place at the right price at the right time. This is their version of a relationship: detailed customer data ready to be monetized into a sale.

Where intimacy once meant a close encounter, it is now a marketing strategy. Companies know everything there is to know about me, the customer: my income level, whether I am a high- or low-maintenance customer, what my buying patterns are, the other kinds of products people like me tend to buy. They know more about my buying patterns than I do. Some day I expect them to know me well enough to send me new clothes that I never ordered. And what bothers me the most is that they will be right: I will probably like what they have drop-shipped to my house.

This form of intimacy could get very expensive. Plus, if they can offer me pants today, can a spouse be far behind?

It says something profound about the nature of our culture when intimacy becomes an instrument of trade. It is interesting that before the term was commercialized, it was not welcome in institutional life. Now that it has lost its original meaning and can be used to sell, it becomes strategic and therefore acceptable.

The Disappearance of Place

When we take the language and knowledge once reserved for close friends and family and, through technology, commercialize it, our sense of place in the world shifts. What we once did with friends, families, and loved ones will now be done with suppliers. Commerce creeps closer and closer to the center of our lives and starts to create an electronic membrane between us and what was once, if not holy, at least human and personal.

The result is that intimacy with the natural and material world is being supplanted by intimacy with the electronic world.

I now spend many hours, even days, learning how to navigate and becoming dependent on this electronic world. I used to be able to set and wind a clock, turn a page in an address book, be surprised by who calls on the phone, cook food over a fire, read by simply turning a page. I could write readable cursive, I could spell, walk down the hall to communicate with co-workers, add, multiply, and divide. Now I can do none of these things. Every time I buy a new labor-saving and life-changing device—which I do because I have a mild addiction to them—I spend hours selecting modes, changing settings, waiting for blinking numbers to calm down, hiding passwords I can never find, and buying batteries.

Technology is amazing, useful, efficient, and at times life saving. But it also has the effect of funneling us into a more virtual way of being and reduces our capacity to live a life that matters. For example, it gives me the illusion of going somewhere. Microsoft asks, "Where do you want to go today?" Well, I am not actually going anywhere. I am sitting right here in front of my monitor. For all its benefits, technology increases my passivity, it isolates me, and it automates more than just my work.

The Illusion of Electronic Reality

I lose touch with myself when I lose touch with what is real, with what is essential about being a person, a part of the earth, intertwined with other human beings. When I become accustomed to a virtual experience, when my private life becomes increasingly organized around my work life, when an electronic world, perfect as it might be, begins to replace my imperfect, decaying, but living and breathing world, I become like that tool.

Here is a summary of the impact our loss of intimacy has on our ability to act on what matters.

The End of the Touch of Reality. When I live a virtual life, in which I can choose my experiences off a menu, I gain the illusion of complete control over my life and those around me, which in clinical terms could be called a mental illness. It is the ultimate state of being out of touch with reality. It is the equivalent of many people's wish to have a garden that requires no maintenance. A friend, Allan Cohen, cleverly argues with my concern by asking why we think that plastic flowers are not real. They *are* real, he says. They are real plastic. You might argue that our electronic experiences are real, they just happen to be electronic.

The End of Nature. In a way, the loss of intimacy in our modern culture is making nature itself obsolete. In agriculture, we have the terminator gene in a seed. This means that the seed is good for only one crop and one harvest. The traditional regenerative power of the seed, as eternal giver of life, has ended. The moment the terminator gene was introduced, the life-giving aspect of nature was ended and now the ability to grant another harvest has been vested in Monsanto and Archer Daniels Midland.

Or consider the way the outdoors is now being manufactured. Go to Las Vegas or the Opryland Hotel in Nashville. They both essentially replace the out-of-doors by covering it on a grand scale. You leave the hotel, walk outside, down a street, and discover that what you thought was outside is just a large dome that covers the immediate world. In this simulated world, the temperature is always 71 degrees, it never rains, and the sun is never in your eyes. I remember going to a restaurant in Las Vegas where we were asked whether we wanted indoor or outdoor seating. We chose outdoors and they seated us on the patio: nice evening, stars above, last light of day slowly fading, quiet breeze from the southwest. Then we suddenly realized we were under a big dome. The twilight, the stars, the breeze were all part of a manufactured natural setting. Who needs nature when you can get a night like this?

Leveraged Learning. Computers and long-distance technology are changing our classrooms and conference rooms. Learning is essentially being "leveraged." Long-distance learning is automating the college campus and the classroom. My favorite teacher now will be someone I have never met. We will be taught by a "master teacher" in a remote location. The possibility of the master teacher in one location, broadcasting their wisdom and knowledge to a thousand other locations, is a growth industry. It is a case of confusing learning with information exchange. Long-distance learning devalues the intimacy of the traditional teacher-student relationship. If we believe that all learning is social and thereby intimate then learning becomes one more way our desire for efficiency and economic value replaces our need for human connection.

Digital Activism. Our capacity for intimacy is also threatened by the way electronic technology substitutes for social and civic engagement. I think I can get all I need from my home entertainment center and never leave the house, meet my neighbors, know my local government. Part of the problem is that the technology is sold as a creator of community. What is the value of connecting with people in China if I never go next door or downtown?

Technology increases our isolation while at the same time promising to overcome it. My mother used to keep the TV on all the time to try to overcome her loneliness. It didn't. It only made enough noise so that she did not have to really make contact with others who might have offered some genuine relief.

▼

Like our idealism, intimacy is needed to keep acting on what matters. We have to make a special effort to deepen our direct participation in the world. This is not an argument against technology, only that it is not a substitute for direct contact. The final cost of virtual connection is that it experientially isolates us and leaves us dependent on a reality constructed by others. It reduces our willingness to show up and invest in the realization of our desires. Our desires are given life by their demand for touch, vulnerability, disclosure, surprise, and raw feeling. Not great conditions for bottom-line bargaining in an instrumental culture. Intimacy is also about more than a relationship. It is the wonder and connection to the earth, to humanity at large, and to something more important than anything that can easily be talked about. It is something that is not knowable or manageable. It must be chosen for the sheer experience of it or it loses its quality. This is what acting on our deeper purpose entails, and operating in an environment of isolation and virtual experience makes acting on a set of values more difficult.

depth

enduring the depth of philosophy. If acting on what matters needs idealism and intimate contact, it also calls us to go deeper into ourselves and become more reflective towards what we most care about. This includes giving ourselves time and space to think independently and to value the inward journey. Without the willingness to go deeper, there is little chance for any authentic change.

We are out of the habit of thinking and questioning; we prefer action and answers. Our favorite clichés express our preference for doing and our ambivalence towards reflection and inwardness:

- We want to have a bias for action.
- It is not enough to simply talk, we want to walk it.
- Talk, after all, is cheap. Actions speak louder than words.
- Don't just stand there, do something!
- In the end, the proof is in the pudding.
- Those who can, do. Those who can't, teach.
- We want a bird in the hand, who cares about the two in the bush? (I wonder how the birds feel about this.)

Intellectual pursuits are not popular in our modern culture. We have negative images of those who spend their lives trying to understand. We condemn thinking by demeaning the "ivory tower." Anyone who values thought over action gets labeled with such terms such as pie-in-the-sky, dreamer, idealist, navel gazer. Serious thought, and the time and depth this requires, becomes a luxury, an impractical distraction.

Inner Space

Thinking, reflection, and going deeper take time and require us to get personal—to question our own beliefs, theories, and feelings. When we decide to set aside time to think, to reflect, we get nervous. The fear is that if we took the time for questioning, for thought, for introspection, we might not have what it takes to act or do. Ours is not to wonder why, ours is but to do or die. Interesting message: If you question, you die.

It is hard to imagine making any important change in life without an inward journey. Think of Christ going into the desert for forty days. It was in the desert that he dealt with his own doubts and temptations and from which he emerged having chosen his freedom and his destiny. It is in our own internal deserts that we remember what really matters. It is on the inward journey, taken over time, that we develop the capacity for intimacy with ourselves and with others, with the environment, and with the world. It is deciding that we are deep human beings with inner lives that defines who we are and brings our ideals back into focus. To put this on a schedule is to undermine the possibilities open to us. We might be willing to go into the desert for five days—who can spare forty days with so much to do and so little time to do it all? There are many things in this culture that make it difficult for us to go deeper; the one I want to focus on is our relationship to speed.

Speed Is God and Time Is the Devil

We are well acquainted with the value of speed. The information age has built its reputation on it. The importance of being first to market, the importance of quick cycle time, turn on a dime, a 24/7 response, we will be there any time, any place, with any thing you need. Just call.

Depth becomes a victim of this love affair with speed. As with most aspects of modern life, what began as a requirement of commerce has expanded and bled into the fabric of our lives. There are legitimate needs for speed, such as in emergencies, or in markets where being first is everything. These legitimate needs, however, often expand to illegitimately change every aspect of our lives—including how we think about what is real and who we are. In this way, speed becomes the antithesis of depth, perhaps even a defense against it.

Some popular examples of the modern, 24/7 life:

- I eat fast food. Perhaps gourmet, low-fat, high-quality, out-of-the-freezer fast food—but it's still fast.

- When I do go to a sit-down restaurant, it becomes a call center.

- I am always on call and my home has become a workplace.

- My belt has become a hanger for pagers and phones.

- Packages and mail come overnight, even though I ignore them for days after they arrive.

- I have no time to read, so I digest everything in sound bites and executive summaries.

Speed and the Quality of Experience

When speed becomes the measure of performance it governs the way we experience our lives as well as the quality of our lives. Speed becomes a reason to settle for lower quality and ignore our desires. A friend, Meg Wheatley, told me about a poet who agreed to publish a poem on a very tight deadline. When she asked how he could do that, he said, "All I have to do is lower my standards."

As an expression of this temporal materialism, we believe that we must postpone what matters until later in life. Young people believe that they need to make money first, and then do what will have meaning. They do this by getting on the "fast track." Living out a set of ideals, doing what I want, making deeper contact with the world, and really engaging those around me—all get postponed.

Artificial Scarcity

The question is whether the need for speed is real or manufactured. In many ways the shortage of time is an artificial scarcity. We think we are increasing the value of time when we make it more scarce than it objectively is. Why have we come to the point where we think there is not enough time? We know exactly how much there is. We do not know when we will die, true, but the number of hours in a day is completely predictable and easily managed. Yet we seem to fight time and the clock.

The marketplace demand for speed may be a realistic standard for production, but who said it had to become a standard for living? Why is speed a god and time the devil? Do we really believe that to have time on our hands is to flirt with the devil.? When did it become a mistake to walk—slowly—instead of ride? When did we decide that there should be a minimum speed on the highway? We end up using speed to fight the devil of free time, unstructured experience, aimless ambling, and the emptiness and lack of direction that exists in each of our lives. Perhaps speed fills a void for us so we do not have to struggle with ideals, intimacy, and depth.

We also treat time as a fact, rather than a perception. In reality, we decide how long fast or slow is. In a doctor's office, time creeps along; when we are in love, days fly by.

If we want depth, we need to step out of time.

The quality of our experience is not measured by the seconds on the clock, but by the timelessness of our experience. We fool ourselves if we ask how long it will take before we know who we are, become conscious, identify with our purpose, or remember our own history in a more forgiving way.

The things that matter to us are measured by depth. Would you assess your humanity by its pace? When I view myself as a time-sensitive product, valued for what I produce, then I have made depth, extended thought, and the inward journey marginal indulgences. Instead of doing what matters, I spend my life doing what works. It increases my market value and postpones the question of my human value.

No wonder we feel lost, or at times helpless, because speed is indifferent to its destination. We are in as much of a hurry to do things that have no meaning as we are those things that actually matter. At times, the only goal is to go faster. Acting on what matters means knowing the difference between moving quickly and knowing where we are going. I know that when I am driving and I am lost, I always speed up. If I do not know where I am going, or if I am going to the wrong place, I want to get there more quickly. This would suggest that speed itself is an indication that we are lost.

▼

If we decide to act on what matters, then we shift our consciousness about pace. There is always time to do everything that really matters: If we do not have time to do something, it is a sign that it does not matter. If we claim that going fast is not our choice, but is a dictate of the world, then we have yet to claim our freedom and risk the possibility of saying no. If we love going fast and speed is our friend, then we need to ask what we are postponing. There is simply no way to shorten the time that depth requires. Any of the values we hold dear wilt under the pressure of time. It is difficult to imagine instant compassion, instant reconciliation, or instant justice. If we yield to the temptation of speed, we short-circuit our values. Ultimately we become disappointed and lose faith in our attempt to bring our strategies and models into the world.

the requirements

This section is about ways to detach ourselves enough from the power of the culture to have an outside—or, more accurately, an outsider's—chance of bringing our intentions into being. The "requirements" are more a way of thinking than a list of things to do. My presumption is that we have all the skills, the tools, the training that we need. Plus, we probably already have the leadership from others that we deserve. In the face of all the messages that the culture sends our way, we can choose to become full citizens and become a cause rather than an effect. This means we must act as if our institutions are ours to create, our learning is ours to define, the leadership we seek is ours to become. It means releasing ourselves from the grip of our ambition and deciding to care for something large enough to give greater purpose to our work and to our experience.

citizen

claiming full citizenship. Our workplaces are major testing grounds for the expression of our values because they are not designed to affirm idealism, invite more intimacy, or encourage depth. In fact, they are breeding grounds for barter, virtual technology, and speed. If we want a shift from focusing on methodology to focusing on purpose, we will have to bring it to work.

Acting on what matters is the act of making change in the world through a set of personal values that define who we are. These values reside beneath the clothing of personality, style, vocation, and the myriad other features that are visible to others. The next few chapters offer ways of rethinking our relationship to our workplace, ways to step outside the patriarchal mindset that still characterizes most of our organizations, despite years of sincere efforts to change it.

The discussion applies to all of us—core workers, supervisors, and senior executives—because the struggle for our freedom does not get any easier as you move up the organizational ladder. Those at the top of the hierarchy are as constrained by it as those entering it today, perhaps more so. The belief that top management is free, and the middle and bottom are not, is pure fantasy. The top may be rich and powerful, but they struggle as much as anyone with finding their own voice, their own purpose, and their own value.

Defining Ourselves as Citizens

To be a citizen, in the political sense, is to have voting rights, membership rights, and the right to create systems that support, not deny, our freedom. In the workplace we do not have the right to elect our leaders, and I do not suggest this. We do, however, vote with our feet, our hearts, our energy, and our care or indifference toward how the institution fares in the world.

We must decide whether to give full service or lip service. We may be called employees, but we can choose to define ourselves as citizens.

Deciding to act as citizens means we are the cause of our environment, not the effect of it. We are not consumers of the organization, waiting to see what management has in mind for us, or wants to sell us. We decide what this place will become. As citizens we have the capacity to act on ideals, to be intimate, and to go deeper, even if our institutions don't reward it.

I entertained the idea of calling this chapter "Growing Up," but the term seemed a little wrong and carries its own baggage. Part of growing up means realizing we are on our own and this calls us to see what is around us with as few illusions as possible. Citizenship means we have claimed our political rights, while growing up is about our emotional freedom. Maybe the unvarnished meaning of growing up is the acceptance that living out our values, and also winning the approval of those who have power over us, is an unfulfillable longing. When we grow up emotionally, or claim our citizenship politically and organizationally, we lose the protection of the parental world.

Acting on what matters means that we will consistently find ourselves feeling like we are living on the margin of our institutions and our culture. This calls for some detachment from the mainstream. It means we have committed ourselves to a state of eyes-open innocence designed to change the world we have inherited. The dominant culture will never fully appreciate the choice we make. This is the cost of citizenship, it is neither free nor cheap. It is a counter-cultural path, treating our work life and personal life as experiments of personal accountability.

Willing to Be Radical

> *The radical, committed to human liberation, does not become the prisoner of a "circle of certainty" within which reality is also imprisoned. On the contrary, the more radical the person is, the more fully he or she enters into reality so that, knowing it better, he or she can better transform it. This individual is not afraid to confront, to listen, to see the world unveiled. This person is not afraid to meet the people or to enter into dialogue with them. This person does not consider himself or herself the proprietor of history of all people, or the liberator of the oppressed; but he or she does commit . . . to fight at their side.*

—Paolo Freire, *Pedagogy of the Oppressed* (p. 21)

Freire's call to arms for full citizenship is a strong statement. Most of us do not think of ourselves as radicals fighting oppression. The oppression that we might consider, however, are those things around us that do not support the values we care most about. There is much in our collective lives that does not support freedom, or compassion, or creativity, or justice. To be radical is simply to find a way of thinking that is unique to each of us. Acting on what matters will place us in the radical's position as soon as we create our own way of affirming our deepest values. Accepting risk and discomfort is what growing up means. Full citizenship in a high-control institution and culture will always be a radical act. Our challenge is to find a way of being radical that eliminates the violence and egoism that has come to be associated with the term.

This is easier said than done. Just because we talk about growing up into full citizenship does not mean that we have experienced it. I have grown older, but am not sure I've grown up. In fact, for much of my early life I didn't want to grow up. Being grown up seemed like an unbearable burden. The grownups I knew seemed weighed down with responsibility and appeared to be in a mild state of depression. As a child, I had to live with the fact that grownups had the power, and they didn't use it to my liking. I also associated being grown up with the loss of dreams, which seemed like a huge liability. It represented a loss of freedom that began with coming of age and ended with being responsible. And growing up appeared to require that I leave the world of natural impulse and do whatever it took, first and foremost, to make a living. I knew the economist and engineer ruled, and I knew that I must become their subject.

Looking back, I think I had it about right. But only about. What I could not see was that the willingness to bear the burden of being adult—of claiming the rights and responsibilities of full citizenship in the world—did not necessarily mean the end of my dreams. It did not require abandoning my ideals or sacrificing my freedom or disengaging from my connection with those around me. It only seemed that way. In fact, at some point in my mid-thirties, my dreams were transformed into a sense of purpose. Still, it had always been a struggle for me to see the possibility of finding freedom that I thought was only available by not being responsible—in other words, by not growing up. Oblivious to the advantages of adulthood, I wanted to stay a child as long as possible, and I have been rather successful at that. It is one of the highlights of my resume.

Creating the World

Growing up means seeing the world as it is. Really growing up means realizing that the world really may be as I see it. Seeing the world as it really is becomes a two-sided coin: It is an honest look at what is out there, and it is knowing that whatever meaning I give to the world is for me to decide. The world comes to me as a fact, but I decide what to conclude from there.

This is not a Zen thing, it is just a complicated thing. Here is a summary of what it means to hold onto the idealism of a child while bringing it into the consciousness of an adult citizen:

1. We continue to articulate our own intentions and dreams. We hold onto the voice of our own desires. This means we stop identifying so strongly with what we do, and stay focused on who we are. The question "What do I do next?" is not a question about desire; it draws us back into method. Only the clear intention of who we are, with whatever degree of clarity we have at the moment, can replace the effort the culture makes to define us by what we do, or by what we are good at. The culture is not going to change unless we deliberately pursue our intentions. It still may not change, but at least we will have stopped digging the hole.

2. We trust our own eyes and intuition. We see things for what they are. This means we are willing to see the world as it is, not as it is presented to us. The painful part is feeling the suffering within us and seeing the suffering around us clearly, and not rationalizing it away—even if we are unable to change it. This requires a certain tragic sense of life. Positive thinking too easily becomes a form of medication. The more we have to remind ourselves to think positively, the more immersed we are in the business of denying our despair at the struggles we see around us.

We decide to move far enough to the edge of the culture to see it clearly. What is the norm and normal does not serve us well. Many of us have tried hard to live a "normal" life, and how is it going? I have taken vows that I have broken, I have hurt people that I have loved, and there is no self talk that will change that. If I can accept these struggles in myself, then my chances of seeing the struggles of others compassionately increases. This means we have to be willing to be abnormal and imperfect. We have to be willing to see clearly and to question what others seem to condone. Any answer given by the dominant culture will never suffice.

3. We become the subject, not the object. We act on our freedom more aggressively. We recognize the difference between being a citizen and being a consumer. The difference between subject and object. Citizens have the capacity to create for themselves whatever they require. Citizens have power, customers have needs. We have been reduced, like bones in a stock pot, to beings with a set of needs to be satisfied. We have desires, not needs—and we can satisfy our own desires. Needs give rise to products that create the illusion that they can give us what we desire. Consumers surrender their freedom for the sake of convenience, safety, personal gain, superiority, pleasure, material value. Pretty appealing, but not worth the price.

So we act as citizens, being accountable for reconstituting the world around us. This means we stop complaining. Complaining is the voice of our helplessness. For example, we love to complain about government. If we grew up, we would stop this. There is no reason to complain about government because a citizen owns and creates the government. Government is there to do the things we cannot do for ourselves. When we complain about government, we are complaining about ourselves. It is *our* government and when we become responsible for our own safety, our own neighborhood, our own children's education, we will stop complaining.

4. We search for intimacy. We seek to reestablish an intimate connection to the world. We see our institutions as an expression of ourselves and so act to humanize them. We know how important it is that the room we inhabit has signs of life. Of nature. We claim nature as our own and move away from simulated versions of it. We do not have dinner in glass-domed villages, we want to know what the weather outside is like. We care about the environment in small and large ways, for the boundary between our own body and the external world is arbitrary.

This also means I pay attention to the details. Why hand them over to the devil? It is the small moments—the way a question is phrased, the quiet voice of doubt in another, the feeling of discomfort with a decision, the nonverbal messages in front of me— that are clues to what matters. Our values are lived out in small ways and if we miss the details, then we lose the values.

5. We choose activism. We dive into the world and swim beneath the surface. We become activists, moving out of electronic enclosures into the neighborhood, into the community, acting to raise the consciousness of everyone we contact. We are a convening agent of human beings in human settings. Wherever people gather, first and foremost, we connect them with each other. We are peers joining together to change the world, not individuals negotiating with our leaders. We become expert at facilitating large-group methods, so that vision, strategies, and accountability are chosen by communities of people answerable to one another. These are strategies of engagement that lead to change. The key is to go more deeply into whatever question we confront, and to do it with other people whenever we can. This means we structure time for reflection, for the exchange of doubts, for considering what really does matter to us. Perhaps we decide to write in a journal instead of making a list of action steps. The actions that matter to us most are the ones we will remember. What is critical is to choose activism and depth as our strategy. This is Paolo Freire's call to arms: to fulfill our capacity to change the world we have inherited and do it by transforming ourselves.

6. We expect our values to be embodied in all that we do. We do not check them at the door when we go to work. What matters most to us is possible as well as important. Let our lives exemplify what we believe in. This means there must be room for uncertainty, and we must also accept the fact that more tools and methodology will not help. What matters to us does not suffer from lack of knowledge or skills. To say we need more skills before we can do anything is usually an excuse. We must keep learning, true, but as we will see later, it is the humanities that we lack, not more technical training.

▼

What all this requires is a shift in our thinking, even though eventually it must be translated into our actions. If we can- not embrace or identify with terms such as radical, or activist, or citizen, our actions will simply be more of the same. Our first order of business is to decide that our deeper purpose will only find expression

when we transform the culture and institutions that we have inherited. This is what
it means to be a citizen, and to grow up.

home
school

home school yourself. When we decide to exercise our freedom and come into our own as full citizens, we rightfully worry about doing it well. The argument for not asking How? is to acknowledge that our problem is not a lack of tools. We have more tools than we need, many of them we will never use, so why keep enlarging the workshop instead of producing something we are proud of?

Just because we stop buying tools doesn't mean we stop learning. Instead of learning about more tools, we need to educate ourselves in a broader sense of the word. I need to become a well-educated person, as opposed to a well-trained person. This means reflecting upon and deepening my own ideas, and giving greater value to my own thinking. It may be that changing my mind is what will lead me to act more fully on what matters. We each have our own theories and models about the world and what it means to be human. We need to deepen our understanding of what we believe. We need a learning curriculum that we, alone, have designed. We need a self-designed course in the "humanities," for we operate in human systems, regardless of how technical and automated they become.

We are not very well equipped to do this, however, because many of us used our education just to build a resume. We got practical way too soon. When people kept asking us what we were going to do with our lives, we thought we needed to give them an answer. Now we need to become clearer on what we are, and what we stand for, not what we want to do, or how to get somewhere.

Humanities Home School

Imagine a humanities home school or graduate program, with yourself as both the student and the core faculty. I like the term *humanities* because this is the quality of the world we want to inhabit. It is our humanity that needs attention. I am not necessarily talking about the humanities that higher education currently offers, but the word that captures the spirit of what higher education stood for when it was (and still is in many places) committed to developing the whole person instead of just the working person. The humanities recognize that the ideas we need today have a long and noble tradition of looking to the arts, drama, literature, religion, and political theory for insight about individual and institutional transformation. Here are some elements for a plan to move in that direction.

The Home School Curriculum

Objective: To act on what matters.

Goals:

1. Hold to the set of ideals that are uniquely mine and have always been with me. No recent imposters based on fashion trends or catchy phrases.

2. Accept that I am now free, a citizen in good standing, and decide to pay the price for that fact.

3. Become intimate with what I come in contact with. See, feel, touch, yield to it all.

4. When in doubt, choose to go deeper rather than faster. Accept the idea that reflection and understanding my own nature, including the dark side, is the key to effective action.

5. Make the world better through activism and engagement. Be on the stage, not in the audience. Change the world through peer groups and community. Let the leaders be.

Course 101: Following Your Heart's Desires

Begin with yourself. Let your desires lead you. Each of us has within us a calling, something that pulls us. We don't really know where it comes from, we don't know whose voice is speaking, and we have no idea what it will eventually demand of us. It is there in the dreams we once dreamed, it is in whatever draws our attention. We get clues about our desires by noticing where our natural energy goes. What would we rather be doing when we are busy not doing what we are supposed to do? People ask me, What are you doing now? I answer, I am busy not answering email. Our desires often come to us in disguise, accompanied by the belief that they are something we cannot make a living at. Good sign.

Three Seconds Remaining in the Game, Our Team Down by One. We find our desires within our own history. If you want a guide, find one—a good therapist, a local artist, it can be anyone outside the field of your current endeavor.

One day it dawned on me in the middle of my life that I had lost my body. I had become, literally, disembodied. I spent my youth wanting to be an athlete. In grade school all I wanted to do was shoot baskets. Hour after hour, often alone, I got lost in my imagination of high drama and personal heroics. My mother would call me in to dinner at 5:00 PM, and not once did I ever go in without first winning a basketball game in the final three seconds.

Despite the legendary feats I had created in my own mind, I had this small problem: I was not that good at basketball. I was slow, I couldn't jump, and the other guys were much stronger. As I moved into high school and college I quietly put my body aside and got on with the business of thinking about starting a family and making a living as best I could. I never stopped wanting to be an athlete, I just gave up on it. In my mid-thirties, when the questions about making a living began to be answered, I started to despair that the rest of my life would simply be the same, just more of it.

To try and deal with this feeling, I bounced around a lot, attending workshops, getting into therapy, trying to Be Here Now with Ram Dass. Then I read a book that took me back to my earlier desire of being an athlete and I began to imagine taking it seriously again. I found Tim Gallwey, author of this great book I had read, *The Inner Game of Tennis,* and asked to be his student. He took me on, and I, in turn, invited him into my work. His gift to me was to bring the world of work and the world of the body together. On the surface I was learning to play tennis, but underneath I was getting acquainted with my own physical nature.

To be an athlete meant to reenter my body. It required me to remember that I had a body and that it had treated me quite well, despite my years of neglect. The goal was not that I would eventually become a great athlete, only that I would refocus my attention. It gave me a clue about what I wanted to learn. What I needed to discover was that learning (the business I was in) was about surrender, trust in myself, faith in my own capacities, and the idea that the best teacher did the least teaching. These were things I had always believed, I just did not fully connect them with the way I had been doing my work. This gave me a way of doing my work that was a fuller expression of my own values. What I ended up learning had nothing to do with tennis. But tennis, the remnant of my earlier desire, became the vehicle that activated my energy and helped bring me back to life.

Knowing More Than You Think. What is interesting is that no matter what you think you want to pursue, you learn the same things about yourself: You learn to pay attention, you experience the power of concentration, you start to notice the details in things that before were undifferentiated masses. You discover how much depth there is in the world and how, when you give it attention, it rewards you. You learn to trust yourself—your body, your instincts, your intuition, your capacities. You learn that you knew more about the subject than you thought you did, and you learn that you are capable of learning. Some of us learn we have a brain, others learn we have a body, some learn we have a voice, or feelings, or the capacity for love, or surrender, or courage, or eyes with which to see. These are the things that are necessary to complete us.

These lessons are what our desires teach us. They are the domain of our desires. We can learn these things everywhere, as long as we stay in charge and stay responsible for our learning. I took a cooking class in the beginning of those restless years (which, incidentally, have not ended) when I started to have to make meals for my children. I went into the class barely knowing how to make hamburgers and spaghetti. For three days I frantically took notes and missed most of what was taught. (I also had fun because we got to eat what we prepared and drank a lot.) A month after the class, someone asked me what I had learned, and I said that I learned to trust myself cooking: I was not a hopeless case, and realized I knew my way around the kitchen better than I thought I had. I learned that to cook you don't need a recipe, you need an eye, a nose, and to be able to tell the difference between vinegar and oil.

Now, the chef did not teach this, the course did not promise this, and I did not go there for this. But this is what I learned. What struck me was that the insight I got from the cooking class was the same thing people often said they got out of any decent training experience. It made me more humble about my work, and over time I realized that the content does not really matter; something else is at work when people decide to show up, listen to their own desires, and be in a situation with not too much teaching but plenty of space for learning.

This means that despite content, it is the act of learning—mostly about ourselves—that is the key to our contribution to, and our ability to make a difference in, the world. Specifically: It is learning about our capacities, strengths, and gifts that are already implanted. Our desires, often masked by our sophistication, point the way.

Course 102: Learning About Ideas Outside Your Field

Whatever our profession, it has little more to teach us. We need a liberal education, not a professional education. I have to go outside my job territory to change my mind. It is hard to learn when we think we know something. Our expertise becomes a defense against the innocence and not-knowing that learning requires. Stop reading professional journals, especially the ones you have to force yourself to read. If you must support your profession, better to write for professional journals than to read them. If you insist on attending a professional workshop, teach it instead.

It doesn't matter what field you learn about, just find something that draws you in and offers the possibility of shifting or deepening your thinking. Go to the liberal arts. If you have already been there, go back to them. Study something, anything. It is the act of learning that is transforming. If you think you don't have time, or love totally what you are doing, or can't keep up with what you are into now, think again. You are hiding from a deeper excursion into your own possibilities. Anytime we think we have it together—that we are on the path and only need some fine tuning—we are stuck. Frozen. Even if all is well, there is a future to create that we have barely dreamed of. We have become imprisoned by our success, caught in the paradox of valuing what we have become, believing that we have all that is required, yet still knowing very little. It is never too early, or too late, to change your mind.

Required Reading. Here are a few books to get you started learning outside your field. They cover a wide spectrum, and if I were the dean, I would make them required reading for meeting the humanities home school degree requirements. They are an excursion across philosophy, revolution, literature, social change, cultural criticism, and architecture. Order them today. Read them tomorrow. Report back to me at the end of the week.

> **Christopher Alexander** A TIMELESS WAY OF BUILD-ING. Brings the quality of being alive into architecture and the built environment. Vivid expression of someone who has acted on what matters. Written in a way that exactly expresses his theory.

> **Marshall Berman** ALL THAT IS SOLID MELTS INTO AIR. Beautifully written insights into the origins of our modern culture. Cuts across literature, economic development, community, institutions, and the individual psyche in a breathtaking way.

> **Wendell Berry** LIFE IS A MIRACLE. Berry writes essays about the community and family costs of industrial society, big universities, powerful government. From a great and prolific writer, this recent book argues for the existence of mystery and wonder in the face of a science-driven culture.

> **Paolo Freire** THE PEDAGOGY OF THE OPPRESSED. This is a classic for all who care about justice and cultural

change. Freire's life was a testament to purpose and service. He dramatizes how each of us adopts the mindset of those who have control over us. Very relevant to organizational life.

Ivan Illich DISABLING PROFESSIONS or MEDICAL NEMESIS. Illich is the most independent thinker I have ever read. His ideas turn everything around. His work ranges from the illness-creating effects of medicine, to reflections on the fourteenth century, to how the introduction of flush toilets created the class structure in Mexico City.

Peter Koestenbaum LEADERSHIP: THE INNER SIDE OF GREATNESS. Peter frames our questions in a way that confronts the difficulty of life and offers immense hope, all in the same sentence. His work ushers in the value of philosophy in creating high-performing leaders. He has helped form the basis of my work over the last twenty years.

John McKnight THE CARELESS SOCIETY. Compelling arguments about the loss of community in our culture. It is also about how efforts to help have the opposite effect and how helpers focus on deficiencies as a way of creating demand for their service.

Robert Sardello FACING THE WORLD WITH SOUL. Another well-written book that brings society together with concerns for the soul. It is a series of letters that will open your eyes and support the importance of bringing your values into the world. This book has elements of psychology, mysticism, religion, spirituality, and anthropology. This size fits all.

When you finish these books for the second or third time, read everything these authors have written. Then find the authors and ask to study with them, or find those who studied with them, and follow the path of their thinking. These books represent the importance of ideas and of thinking. I am not sure, but I do not think there is one list of how to do it in any of these books. Amazing.

Course 103: Mentoring on Your Own

Mentoring is an act of love, of care, of willingness to bear witness for another human being. To be authentic, it must be chosen by both parties. It happens to us as much as it is a goal that we pursue. Once it becomes popular, a learnable skill, and an organizational project, it loses its life. So, don't look to your boss to be a mentor. Find a mentor on your own. You boss may be a great mentor, but your boss has power over you, and this gives an edge to the guidance offered. And if you want to fire your boss as a mentor, you have to do it indirectly and with difficulty. Plus, you don't want to love your boss—it would be too close to the parenting experience that our freedom wants us to grow up and away from.

There is unquestionable value in mentoring, but we get into trouble when it becomes a program and our bosses are trained and expected to do it. Employees then begin to think they need to be mentored or have a right to be mentored. When mentoring becomes a product it turns from care to entitlement. So stop supporting mentoring programs. Just find a person, whether you know them or not, and make them a mentor, even if you never meet them. I have mentors whom I have never met, but I follow everything they write, do, and say. If you do meet, it is a bonus, but be sure the relationship is reciprocal. You need to have something to offer your mentor in return for learning from them. If there is no balance, the relationship will become unstable, even a little oppressive. Both of you need to be transformed by the process of learning from one another. People sometimes ask me to be their mentor, and I ask them what I might receive from this arrangement. They respond that I get the benefit and joy of seeing them grow. I think of saying, "But I already have enough children." Making unbalanced, burdensome demands on others keeps us in the child position.

In the workplace, the risk is that we become too willing to let others define for us what we should learn. The colonial nature of organizations is most visible when leaders think they (we) know what is best for others. We are still are too eager to ask our bosses for feedback, to ask them how we are doing, what we should be learning. These are great conversations, but not with people in power, for the discussion can become instrumental all too easily. We try to get what we want from the boss by positioning ourselves as eager students. The boss is trying to get what they want from us under the guise of learning, generosity, and acting in the best interest of the employee.

We are so conditioned by our school experience that we think we need this kind of direction and prescription. All through school we put our energy into reading the teacher. The first questions are "What do you expect of us? What does it take to get an A?" The dependency runs so deep that if you are a college professor, like David Cox at Arkansas State, and try to renegotiate the learning contract with students, you are in for a battle. Students don't want to hear about adult learning theory, setting their own goals, devising their own grading system, or being responsible for the learning of their peers. They want an A. It is made worse when the professor who tries to bring democracy into the classroom has to stand blindfolded in front of the firing squad of student evaluation forms.

Mentoring has meaning when we take on for ourselves the task of learning. And we do it in the face of all the help sent our way. My freedom, my purpose, my learning, are all faces of the same intention: living out my own destiny and bringing this into the world with all the worth and generosity I can muster.

Course 104: Making Peers the Point

A perfect source of learning is our peers. Despite all we know about the power of collaborative learning, we defend against doing this. When we listen to a presentation or a attend a workshop, and the leader asks us to break into small groups, most of us groan. "We didn't come here to pool our ignorance." This says volumes about our lack of appreciation for our peers and our own ideas about learning. When did we conclude that our peers were ignorant? We have been so conditioned to compete against our peers that we have no faith we can learn from them.

All learning is social. It is with our peers that we will ultimately find our voice and change our world. It is in community that our lives are transformed. Small groups change the world. Form one or join one. There are book groups, learning groups, and on-line dialogues everywhere.

Course 105: Treating the Workplace as Classroom

The final course is to view the workplace as a classroom. Not just for you, but for all involved. This is the best kind of experiential education: Let the business take on the purpose of teaching people how to run a business. Each person learns as many different aspects of the business as possible. This signals the end of specialists as they are replaced by full-service entrepreneurs. This is a particularly good strategy for a small business where it is difficult to keep people, pay big bucks, and invest in training. The boss says I will teach you all I know about this business, and we say yes.

If your setting is a large organization, view it as a training laboratory, where people come for a while and leave when their experiment is over. View every job this way. Be curious about it all. It is a great classroom and you can learn even if the boss is not interested in teaching. This also gives purpose to an organization or business. The workplace is an incubator for economic and emotional self-sufficiency.

The Point

Think of all of this as home schooling, where you are the teacher and the student, the parent and the child. Montessori is a good model if you want some ideas and a powerful philosophy about learning. Maria Montessori spent most of her teacher education trying to get teachers to stop teaching. She believed that learning should be self-directed and collaborative. Find your local Montessori school and spend four hours in a classroom once a week for four weeks. You will find an imperfect but inspiring way to think about instruction and learning.

We have to spend a lot of our learning time trusting in what we know and knowing what we believe in. This is the challenge. There are few schools that teach this, which is why we have to create our own, even though it has only one student—you.

▼

At the core, our intent is to learn about things that go deeper than lifestyle and skills. Even though we have all the knowledge that is required to act, it does not mean that we are complete. Or that we should stop learning. It is our freedom that we are learning about, and freedom is a young and awkward child that needs nourishment to keep growing. The fundamental questions are: What do we learn? Who decides this? and Where do we go to learn it? These make a big difference. We need to ensure that the learning process itself is a reflection of the living process we choose.

boss

your boss doesn't have what you want. On his death bed Machiavelli was asked by a priest if he would like to redeem himself by renouncing the devil and his evil ways. "No," he replied. "This is no time to be making enemies."

What Are We Afraid Of?

Let us start with a simple truth. I generally avoid the word *truth* except when it refers to the voice of God. It seems presumptuous to declare anything with such certainty. What is called truth is usually opinion. In this case, however, I am willing to call the following statement a truth:

Most people in organizations are afraid of their boss.

You aren't, but most people are. Now, you may not be afraid of your immediate boss, but move up the chain of command and each of us will find someone to worry about. If you don't want to call it fear, then can you agree that we are very eager to please the boss? We care deeply what the boss thinks, plans, values, and wants. This truth is quite amazing.

Some moments of truth that stay with me:

> **One:** I spent a morning at The Boeing Company with a work unit that was having a weekly team meeting. I had been invited to the meeting by Ralph, who said that he was implementing empowerment with his team and getting great results. Would I like to observe a meeting? Absolutely. So I sat in and was very impressed.
>
> The conversation was free, confronting, supportive, and funny. The manager spoke openly about problems and

mistakes. Results data were shared freely with the group, accountability was quickly taken for disappointments, participation was widespread, and people at every level thought and spoke as though they cared about the business. For this team in this meeting, democracy was intact, partnership was in place. The world was right.

After the meeting I was in the hall talking with Ralph about how special the meeting was, how Ralph understood empowerment and seemed to be living it. Then someone walked up and whispered in Ralph's ear. I saw the expression on his face instantly change. The smile became a grimace, his jaw dropped, his eyes narrowed and glazed over. I asked Ralph, "What's up?" He said his boss wanted to see him. That was it. His boss wanted to see him. He was sorry he had to leave so quickly, would I be all right? Off he went at a slow jog and disappeared up the stairs.

Two: I am at an off-site meeting with the executives of a finance division of a big bank. We are talking and the cell phone of the executive vice president rings. He answers and jumps up all in one motion. In an instant, he is out the door. I ask the others, "What happened?" They say that his two bosses must want something from him, which happens a lot: He is on call and reachable whenever they need him. I ask when he is coming back and what we should do. Although they don't know when he will be back, we should probably wait for him. So eighteen of us wait and wander for fifteen minutes or so until he returns.

When he comes back and we settle down, I ask if there is any chance he can turn off the phone and postpone answering until after the meeting. He says, "No—they expect me to keep it on and answer it right away." This is a very senior executive, on call, 24/7, no questions asked.

There are a hundred more examples of strong, competent people on call and uneasy, and you have your own stories. People are afraid of those above them. When you ask what they are afraid of, they inevitably talk about how the bosses are controlling, impatient, demanding, in crisis, or indifferent, distant, and unreachable.

Pinning the Tail on the Donkey

If the boss has power that causes us concern, we have to consider what we are doing to create that. What power do we give away that interferes with our own purpose? What expectations do we have that lead to fear and caution? Nothing will change until we can accept the fact that the fear we feel is our own creation. Granted, everyone feels it at some point, so it is culturally very common, but it is still ours.

We make the boss powerful because we want something in return. We are so mired in our dependency, we believe that without their support and approval, we cannot get what we want. There are four beliefs we have about bosses that we might reconsider:

1. They hold my future in their hands. They hold the answer to my ambition. After all, they have the authority to reward and punish me with pay, assignments, breathing room, and a smile.

2. They are instrumental to my development. I have something vital to learn, and I need to learn it from them.

3. They create the culture that I live within, and this determines my morale and well being. What they do makes me happy or sad.

4. They have the information I want and need. They are privy to the real story, and they are keeping it from me.

By now, you know where I am going with this, so let me state briefly why these four beliefs make us afraid and give our freedom and sense of purpose away.

Promote Me

On the matter of your future, there is a chapter coming up that tries to convince you to give up your ambition. On the slim chance it is not persuasive, there are three reasons why it is foolish to look to your boss to provide the future you have in mind.

First: There is no rational process whereby people get promoted. When your boss meets with other bosses to promote someone, you really don't know how much influence your boss will have in those discussions. Plus, your future depends on which job is open, who got their person in last time, who is really calling the shots, what the politics of the moment are. You may have worked hard, delivered on your promises, and been selected for the employee highlight film three quarters in a row, yet that may not count—and you can count on that.

Second: Despite all the competency models, objective criteria, and wishes to be fair, judgments about future leaders are made on subjective opinions over which you have no control. There may be something about you that they just do not like. You may have joined in the wrong year. You may be in the wrong function. You may not stylistically fit in with their idea of royalty. When getting feedback from your boss, don't listen too carefully to their improvement suggestions for you. Even if you transform yourself in response to their feedback, it does not mean you are going anywhere. Also, their feedback has little to do with who you are. They are mistaking you for the Ghost of Christmas Past.

Third: There is no place to go. Organizations are flattening, manager jobs are disappearing. Your boss may be the next one to be structured out of a position. Your unit is likely to be matrixed, outsourced, sold, or redeployed into outer space. Don't bet that there will still be a job there when you are ready to move up.

Coach Me

As for needing a boss for our development, we don't. Our development is in our hands and we should keep it there. As stated earlier, the fact that the boss has power over us is in itself an obstacle to learning. And who is to say they see us clearly enough to be helpful? Women are constantly being told they are either too aggressive or too emotional. Men are told they should get better at relationships. Neither assessment is likely to be that true, it is more likely to be a projection of the boss than a description of the subordinate.

You might wish that things were different, that you would get the coach you have been waiting for. But when all is said and done, your boss is not your best source of feedback. It is not that bosses don't wish to be helpful. They do. But they aren't. Of course, all bosses pride themselves on how they help develop people, but this does not make them good at it. Remember that all patriarchs believe in participation, they just feel their particular people aren't quite ready for it.

You may have had a boss that did in fact help greatly in your development, but to keep looking for this is a defense against getting on with it yourself, regardless. Also, much of our suffering comes from having internalized the opinions of others. This was the reality of being a child, when our parents' definition of us was understandably powerful. But to continue this process as an adult is not smart.

Create a Culture for Me

We think that management shapes the kind of culture we live in and thereby determines morale and satisfaction. Or even performance. Does my boss motivate me? Or demotivate me? Am I waiting for my boss to light my fire? What happened to my own matches? Why would we knowingly place our satisfaction and motivation in the hands of another? Of course, our bosses' behavior will make a difference to us, but if they are the cause of our experience, then we have surrendered our freedom. We are meant to be creators of our culture and bring the qualities we want into the world we inhabit. This is the definition of our freedom, and to back away from this keeps us in bondage.

Things get really ugly when people tell us that our job is to make our bosses look good. This is demeaning to us and to them. Are our bosses unable to make themselves look good? And when did we sign up to be a butler, hair stylist, speechwriter, or personal shopper? This sets us up for a covert bargain that is destined to disappoint. If we make them look good, does this then obligate them to take care of us? This culturally supported instrumentality is simply an expression of our cynicism and our vote for a permanently patriarchal world.

Give Me the Real Story

We have so many expectations of our bosses that lead to disappointment, and one of the most common is to constantly think that management is not telling us everything. Most attitude survey results ask management to keep "their people" better informed. If management knows something and is not telling us, it may be because they are worried about our feelings. They have heard our plea for protection and fulfill our request by withholding information that might make us anxious. This is why we may hear about big organizational changes through the media before we are told directly. If we want protection, we will pay the price by living in the dark. The moment we give up the protection, we will get the real story.

The more likely reason we do not hear the real story directly from management is that often they don't know it. They don't know what will happen to us, our unit, our organization. They can't predict the future any better than we can. It is the child in us that believes that our bosses know everything. What we want from them, they just do not have. They aren't keeping anything back from us—any more than we would withhold from our subordinates what they desire. Try to remember that every time we complain about our bosses, our subordinates are making the same complaint about us. Not always true, but a good rule to operate by.

They Are Not Going to Change

Regardless of how much of the above you accept, it is important to accept the fact that they are not going to change. We need to stop expecting it or even working on it. Question Four in the How? family is "How are we going to get those people to ... (you name it)?" The wish to get others to be different is a wish to control them, which in itself creates its own resistance. No matter how beneficial those changes could be to the institution, our efforts to change others make no sense. This is where the culture has it wrong: Although we listen to evangelical pronouncements about how others need to change, there is no evidence that these pronouncements do anything but further alienate those we have in mind.

Also, what does it mean when our bosses become "those people"? Referring to them as "those" is a measure of our contempt and alienation from them. We have decided they are strangers and we claim superiority over them when we label them "those people." And wanting to "get them to..." is an act of aggression, even if our intentions are noble. All the more so if we are consultants, brought in to help, and find ourselves speaking in the alienated language of those we came to serve.

We will better serve our institutions and our own intentions when we get the fact that "they" are not going to get it. And if they did, it would not help us. If they changed their behavior, our questions and doubts would just have to find a new residence. When we believe that our well being is dependent on the transformation of others, we are racing back to the starting line and avoiding our own responsibility.

There Is No One to Blame

Family therapy uses a concept that is useful here: the identified patient. Every family and work team has a member who most think should shape up. If only this person would pull their weight, it would eliminate obstacles for the rest of us.

We think *they* are the problem. We want to fix them or get rid of them. What is interesting is that if we succeed in getting rid of them, within six months someone else takes their place. If we get a new boss, after a six-month honeymoon, we begin to complain. Sometimes the new person we wished for becomes the polar opposite of the one they replaced. If the last boss was too controlling, this one cannot make up their mind. If the last member of the team did not carry their load, this one wants to do it all.

Individuals who seem to be the problem—for a work group or in a family—are a symptom, not the problem. They simply carry and express the problems that we do not want to face. They may be acting out our own lack of clear purpose, our own inability to communicate directly with each other, or our avoidance of holding each other accountable. Instead of facing our own contribution to the problem, we project it onto another. We get a payoff from focusing on their behavior because it distracts us from focusing on our own. It is our own transformation that creates the best climate for change.

As an individual free to create the world we live in, I carry the cause for how my boss and others respond to and treat me. Once I understand this and stop trying to control them, I can get on with the business of acting on what matters. Others, our bosses included, are more likely to reflect on their own behavior as a result of witnessing our self-reflection than yield to our desire for them to be different.

Betrayal and Disobedience

Carl Jung said that disobedience is the first step towards consciousness. Not only are we not here to fear or please our bosses, but we should realize there is meaning and value in our acts of disobedience—not disobedience for its own sake, but as a fuller expression of our own unique humanity and purpose. The fact that we are disappointing authority may be a sign that we have begun to live our own lives, that we have become fully engaged. We do not know that our lives are our own until we have paid for the choices we make. This is choosing adventure over safety. The adventure we can trust is the journey towards our own freedom and our belief in what is real and valuable.

To hold a stance in the face of disapproval means that the ground we stand on is our own. In philosophic terms, it is choosing existential guilt over neurotic guilt. Neurotic guilt is what we feel when we disappoint the expectations of others. Neurotic guilt is a symptom of an inauthentic life, when we ask the culture, by way of a boss or a parent, who we are and what we should become.

In its messages about what is real and what is best, our culture invites us to live a life chosen by others. If we feel guilty for disappointing the boss or the institution, the problem is not our actions, but the conclusions we draw. If we decide we are at fault, or continue to wish they were different and would appreciate us more, we are still living another's life and hoping for a world that does not exist.

Existential guilt is the guilt that comes from having betrayed ourselves. It is the positive force behind our acts of disobedience and efforts to reclaim who we are. This serves our freedom and purpose. Existential guilt is what we feel for not being who we are, for wasting our lives and postponing our own possibilities. This guilt can be ennobling. It draws us towards deeper and deeper integrity and keeps in front of us the task of fulfilling the potential given to us at birth.

Stated simply, this way of thinking offers the redemptive value of betrayal. At some point in our lives, each of us must betray our parents. We acknowledge that we are not the children they had in mind. Period. It frees us to inhabit our own life and also is, incidentally, liberating for our parents, whether they are alive or not, or in contact with us or not. Every parent's deepest wish is that their children are self-sufficient, happy, and able to live a full life. When we say no to a parent, or a boss who serves as a surrogate parent, it liberates them from the confines of the parenting role and, whether acknowledged or not, gives them the satisfaction of playing a role in the recovery of our most precious of gifts, our freedom.

They may not know that our betrayal is a gift. They may not appreciate our disobedience. But our actions carry the unmistakable potential for parents and bosses to work through their own transformation. We, at least, will have done our part in bringing both emotional and political balance into our relationships with authority, and this is the most powerful thing we can do. Especially when we are able to do it in a way that maintains contact rather than alienates others.

> Whatever we do, we cannot control or predict what impact we will have on those around us. This is not the aspect of life to be strategic or tactical about—the engineer is of no use to us here. We hope to find a way to find our own ground that is compassionate and caring. But no one is terribly graceful when renegotiating a relationship. All we can do is act in good faith and forgive ourselves for the clumsiness of our apprenticeship.

It Is My Business

We all live with people who have power over us and we need to come to terms with them. We affirm our own freedom and our commitment to an institution when we look past the behavior of a boss and respond to their intent. We always have the choice to offer the benefit of the doubt, earned or not. We can decide that management has the best interests of the institution at heart and we can work to understand their intentions, even if their tactics do not seem to be aligned with their purpose.

It is not that we need to be correct about the more noble intent of those at the top, but when we make the effort, in that moment we act as an owner of the business and this is always in our best interest. My freedom and fulfillment come from acting to create something that I believe in. I can choose this perspective independently of whether the world supports or rewards or even wants this from me. The questions become "What is the boss trying to do?" and "What is needed now for the well being of the whole?" The follow-up question, always, is "What are we want-ing to create together?" Asking these questions opens up a path-way toward independent action.

Stop Seeking Hope Out There

One final thought about letting go of our leaders: One of the things we want from leaders is for them to offer us a positive vision of the future—in other words, hope. When they do not express hope—as when Jimmy Carter claimed during his presi-dency that the U.S. was in a malaise—we feel angry: How could they let us down like that?

But why should we ask our leaders to define reality for us? Must they carry hope that we cannot sustain? This is the way we ask them to lie to us, and then we blame them for not fulfilling the tomorrow they offered. Anyway, hope is overrated. Werner Erhard claims that hope is a foolish wish, a mistake. He states that hope is the acknowledgment that we are not living into a possible alternative future, we are living in our past. He is wise about this. Hope is the statement of something we do not have. A reproach to our own capabilities.

Our claims of hope or despair are not based on what is out there. They are a projection of our experience, of our own learning. When we are alive and in motion, the world is alive and in motion. When we are digging a hole, hope has forsaken us. It is the projection of the moment.

We are told not to open Pandora's box. We try to avoid disagree-able conversations or experiences. Institutions are clear that there is no room for messy or painful discussions. What a shame, for what resides at the bottom of Pandora's box is Hope. Which means that if we wish to hold on to the idea of hope, it has to be paid for—it must be purchased by the courage to dive when drowning, to go down into the dark, mysterious dimensions of our experience. And if this is valid, the idea that we can receive hope for the price of listening to a leader describe the future is looking for a bargain that has no value.

The same applies to hope's cousins: optimism and pessimism. The external world provides ample data to support either optimism or pessimism, so each becomes a choice. In a scene from *Candide*, in which Dr. Pangloss is surrounded by violence and the loss of life and limb, he declares, "This is the best of all possible worlds." So here we are. There is no such thing as reality-based optimism or pessimism. All we have is the experience of our own vitality or lack of vitality which, when projected onto the world, we may call optimism and pessimism.

▼

If we continue to pursue hope then we had best become a producer of it, rather than a consumer of it. Let it be an offer rather than a demand. Let us offer hope to our leaders, since we create them, because they need all the support they can get. If you supervise others, let them read this chapter. They won't like it, but at least you gave them a warning.

10

ambition

oh, by the way...you have to give up your ambition.

Much of our discussion has been about the price we must pay to act on what matters. The price may seem high for what amounts to an adventure we had not planned on, but then we also pay a price for choosing safety. The safe roads of pragmatism and compliance do not come cheaply, although the promise of our culture is a little more optimistic. The culture offers a special deal on safety. It promises that if we have

- unquestioned loyalty to our organization's goals and culture,
- respect for its leadership,
- a belief that technology, speed, and efficiency are the keys to prosperity,
- and trust that the cream will rise to the top if we keep the faith and are patient ...

... then these things will bring us safety in the form of membership, economic security, and a good life.

This promise fulfills the longing in each of us to be taken to a high lookout by our father and told, "Someday all this will be yours." The only stipulation is that you be a good son or daughter.

We are enjoined to live by these beliefs from the moment we enter school, often from the moment of birth. We believe that these guidelines, or ones like them, provide the cohesion that makes modern society work. This, then, is the life held before us, whether we have a real shot at it or not. This is the blueprint for a consumer society. This is the fuel for our ambition.

The wish for that moment with our father or mother or surrogate, when all will be turned over to us, may be the wish to be blessed by God. If this is the case, then seek what you want from God, but not from a second-level supervisor. Or an organization.

Questioning the Payoff

The promise of full membership and its security is what we have to give up for our genuine freedom, our ultimate security, and a life that matters. Growing up and claiming our citizenship is accompanied by the realization that it is our ambition that leads us into the arms of the culture. I am speaking here of our ambition to rise to a position of institutional power, to be recognized by our profession, to be offered the keys to a gated community. This is the ambition we have to question. Why we have to give up our ambition, I do not quite get, though I know it is true. The choice to not seek societal approval, parental pride, and institutional safety is a very difficult and personal matter. It may be possible to be ambitious and not lose control over our own lives while pursuing the ideals of another, but I have rarely seen it work. Even if attainable, lifestyle and ease are too small gods to worship. As is seeking the answers to How?

Here are some ways that our ambition and willingness to live up to the standards of the culture tend to imprison us:

1. The higher up you go in an organization, the more anxious the people are. Those at the top seem pressured to believe they have the answers and to speak as if everything they say must be quotable. When they give talks, the text is written out for them. When they move through the organization, they rarely do so alone, which makes me think they are a bit lonely and shy. Were they always this way, or did the weight of responsibility transform them?

2. Retirement parties are often the first place where the truth is told in public. They are, for many, the first time that years of caring for the institution and what it stands for are celebrated. This is the time when people are more likely to tell the truth about you (and others) because now their hold on you is over,

you are about to go free. You are no longer vulnerable. You no longer live in the shadow of the sword because you are about to be released. You are finally bulletproof. If you stand up, you might get shot, but you won't feel the pain.

3. The winners in our culture have little capacity to criticize themselves. If we should question the cultural mindset, or the purpose of our institutions, or the role of leadership in our organizations or community, we are reminded quickly that capitalism is the best system ever devised, that our organization has been successful over the years, and that top management has the right idea. There is little room for critique. When we face activists desiring rapid change, we pull back, for they activate our fears of chaos and disarray. This is why we have banished our artists to the fringe of society and tell them to eat cake. It is our artists who choose freedom over safety and use their talent to question and confront the culture.

Doing Good Work

It is important to recognize that giving up ambition does not mean we are giving up desire, just the opposite. Ambition, again, means seeking recognition from our institutions, their leaders, and our profession. We trade ambition for choices about what matters, about how we choose to operate, and about what we choose to create. What is affirmed is our determination to do good work, with or without approval. When we choose this idealism, we negate the mindset that it is human nature to pursue self-interest, that people do mostly what they are rewarded for, and that if something does not get measured, it does not get done.

Giving up our ambition doesn't mean we have to change jobs or go anywhere. We just have to get the point. We postpone the How? questions. We say Yes and get on with it.

Giving up our ambition is not easy. Acting on our values and achieving recognition from the world are both real and universal longings, and both matter. The problem is we must begin with caring about the world, which means acting on our values. The idea is first to embrace the task of reconstituting the world and then hope you get some support for it. It is the reconstruction, or transformation, of the culture by our living example, our words, and our commitments that is our fundamental work. Each of us does it in our own way, and together it becomes a unifying expression of our care, even our love for it all. This is an act of intimacy and the experience of our own depth.

The Boss Is No Motivator

And if you are the boss, stop using your approval with its tacit possibility of advancement as a carrot. As motivators, carrots should be reclassified as a banned substance. Their use is based on research done on naïve pigeons and Pavlov's dog. As we have already seen, the whole idea that bosses should motivate their people ties us all in knots. Instead, bring your employees together and stimulate the right conversation. This is an important role for any boss—to support the communal pursuit of what matters. Let this be motivation enough. Why not operate to support those who experience their freedom and care about the whole? It would be a welcome relief from the despair-ridden discussions about what to do with the dead wood and how to deal with employees crying out to be rescued.

To explore the meaning of ambition as either a boss or a subordinate, ask yourself the questions "If I got what I want, what would it give me?" and, "Is it something that I really want?" and, finally, "Would I take it right now?" I heard these questions from consultant and author Charlotte Roberts, and they took me to an interesting place. Answering them over and over again, each time beginning where the last answer left off, got me closer to what I really want, which for most of us would be to live and experience our deepest values.

Second-Order Ambition

A special note to those who have been dealing with questions like these for a while: Just when you think you have faced your ambitions and reclaimed your true purpose, started valuing relationships, and caring for the whole again, just when you begin to experience some freedom and have gotten into the practice of saying Yes, ambition has a way of sneaking in the back door. For now, as my daughter Jennifer says, we are on the spiritual fast track. We seek proof, recognition, and approval for how together we have become, for how participative we are as managers, for how values-driven we are now, how we are transforming our organization's culture to become agile, quick, employee-focused, customer-based, and shareholder-friendly. Be all these things, but stop claiming credit for them. The credit-claiming and pronouncements are the way marketing and cosmetic refinements replace genuine change.

▼

It's the same for individuals as it is for institutions: The more we focus on what counts to us, the more complicated we realize it is. There is no hurry, no place to go, no destination we will reach in our lifetime. We are there the moment we begin. And each time we strive to be recognized and rewarded we are reminded of the work we have left to do.

whole

care for the whole (whether it deserves it or not).
Growing up and achieving our citizenship papers is marked by a commencement. We have been invited to give the commencement address at our own graduation, the beginning of saying Yes to our own freedom, our own readiness to assume full accountability. Our freedom begins with knowing our intentions, knowing what matters to us, knowing which values will guide our actions. The question, then, is what are we willing to commit to?

A Broken Promise

There was time when the workplace answered the question of commitment for us. At least it did for me. When I began work at Exxon I stepped quite naturally into a social contract. I made a commitment to the company and, in exchange, they made a commitment to my future. The contract was affirmed right in the beginning. In the recruiting interview they asked me predictable questions about how I saw my future and then they talked about how they saw it. If I worked hard, met their objectives, was open to learning, and adapted to their style and culture, the path was clear. In six months I would get a $35 monthly raise (this was a long time ago), in eighteen months I could expect a better job title, in two to two-and-a-half years, a promotion to supervisor. Section head title came after three to five years, but with my potential, it would more likely be three. I was introduced to managers who had moved along this path, role models, the works.

The same afternoon I was taken with my wife on a tour of the area and shown where new employees typically lived, then across the highway where senior staff resided, and then up the hill, ambitiously named the Watchung Mountain, where the executives lived. I didn't exactly pick out a specific house on the hill, but the Tudor with a double garage kind of spoke to me.

All that was left was for me to say yes, which I did after stalling two days to indicate I had other offers and was choosing Exxon for the right reasons.

Soon after I was on board, the oil crisis hit and Exxon had its first-ever layoff at my division—and everything changed forever. It took a few years to realize that this would become a way of life, that the pattern was set. The social contract was broken, the deal was off, and eventually we all knew it. The contract that I would work hard and they would take care of me was broken, and then some.

Commitment without Barter

Here we are in the new century and most of us cannot even remember that contract. We now celebrate the era of free agency. We have taken the negatives of abandonment and betrayal by the companies that employed us and turned them into individual entrepreneurial positives. We are free agents, as in the sports world, which means we sell our services to the highest bidder. I am CEO of I, Inc., and the culture tells me at every turn that my commitment should be to myself, to build my own skills, to market myself as a product, to travel with my pension. If I am an MBA grad from a decent school, I am into exit strategies. Make the money first and then do what matters. Companies, in turn, outsource whatever they can, reduce benefits where possible, make no commitments to employees other than a day's fair pay, or at least a day's pay.

This leaves us having to choose that which, previously, was a given. What do I care about and want to give my best attention to? The culture tells me to manage my career to my own best advantage. The opportunity open to us is to decide to commit to something larger even though there is no promise in return. The economist says don't be a fool. Maximize you, the product. Go with the best offer. If no promise is made, no commitment is required.

> If I listen to the economist, I commercial-
> ize myself and spend my years living an
> instrumental life. If I value my freedom,
> then I must reclaim it sooner rather than
> later. My freedom is expressed by my
> commitments, not from my bargained
> agreements. It is only when I have made
> choices without any expectation of return
> that I know I chose freely. If I commit as
> an act of barter, I have denied my free-
> dom. Thinking of myself as a product, a
> free agent, turns me into a commodity.

This alienates me from my self, it objectifies me, and it happens by my own hand. So an essential step toward choosing Yes is the decision to commit to something larger than me, indifferent to the bargains available to me. Something shifts within me when I commit to an institution with no expectation of return. As long as I am in this job, I will care about this place. The answer to barter is generosity.

The Place Matters

Now the question becomes what I define as "this place." Is it my unit, my team, my organization? The traditional answer to this question is: Identify narrowly and build it well. Steward your unit well, guard your property line well, and the rest will take care of itself. The challenge facing us, that will define us, is how wide a boundary do we draw for ourselves? Who looks after the com-mon ground of the whole institution? The culture says it is top management's job to care for the institution, our job is to focus on the task at hand. Let those above us hold it all together. This is the narrow-interest model.

We need to realize that we may be distrusted and accused of altruism if we demonstrate care for the institution as a whole. We might give back budget money or suggest that some people in our group would do better to report to another manager. We might volunteer that many of the things we do are not worth doing and would best be stopped. To take these actions would be definitely counter cultural, so we have a chance to be a fool. The questions that serve us are What do we care about? and How do we act on that intention, in the face of the cultural messages? and Will we do this with no anticipation of reward and some expectation of contempt? For when we focus on the whole, at the possible cost to our unit, it quietly pressures others to do the same, and this pressure is not welcome. Violating tacit agreements for the sake of the business used to be called rate-busting.

Institutional Purpose

The question of commitment is the same for the institution. It has to decide whose interests it is there to serve. The economist's answer is, "It's the shareholders, stupid!" Economists have even declared that any act of pure social responsibility is against the shareholders' interests, and the owners can take management to court for wasting assets on social concerns.

The question of purpose is more complicated for a not-for-profit, or what some call public benefit, organization. Their mission statement usually involves caring for some common good. But their way of operating has its own boundary questions. Is it a service agency only there to serve its target population? Is it in competition with other agencies for scarce funding? Whom are we here to serve? is the most profound institutional question of commitment. Conventional wisdom places our boundary at the property line. The city line is the boundary for local government, the national border is the limit for world leaders.

For example, take a community center that offers health and recreational services. It has a fitness facility, day care center, and a program of youth activities. Is it in competition with other community centers in nearby towns? Is it in competition with private fitness centers and private day care centers? Most of its employees believe they are in competition and act accordingly. They think that their objective is to be the Number One community center in the region.

Instead, why not decide that its mission is to support community everywhere, to support fitness wherever people choose to work out, to support day care for all families who need it?

This would indicate that the center's real purpose is to act on a set of values about interdependence, civic engagement, family, health, and caring for the next generation. If we were to take these values seriously, we would believe that we have a stake in the success of all community centers, fitness facilities, and day care operations. We would create an alliance of these other organizations and work to improve them all. We would look at the strengths of each operation and have the best teach the rest. We would share operating information and perhaps have overlapping board memberships to support the younger or struggling centers.

The marketing strategy would be to get more people exercising, more kids cared for, more community involvement in the area. The community center I have in mind has 2,000 members. All the community centers, fitness centers, and day care facilities in the region have about 8,000 active members. There are 75,000 people living in the region. Why not say that the marketing goal is to get another 10,000 people actively participating, regardless of where they go?

Now you might say that most organizations already belong to an association that promotes their interests. But most associations protect the boundaries of their individual members rather than overlap and expand their boundaries. Few "competitors" are committed to each other's success. The shift to Yes would be to take seriously the service and values mission of the institution, and treat more casually its boundaries and domain. The climate for this kind of thinking is increasingly receptive with the increase of alliances and partnerships, but the mindset of "This is my unit, my division, my organization" is still strong. It is interesting that when we seriously suggest a wider notion of what is "ours," we are told that we are too idealistic. To which I would say, Thank you!

If I keep the boundary line at what I own, then no one is attending to the common ground and it grows fallow. In the economist's mind the free market will take care of that. Survival of the fattest. Could it be that the ground has value for its own sake, not for its economic potential?

Good Fences Make Poor Neighbors

The classic response to ideas like these is a mixture of cynicism and fear. If we advocate giving away what we own, yielding on our own economic interests, caring for something for its own sake, we are asked to justify it as being in the best long-term interests of the institution. Or of the individual. Self-interest, whether short or long term, is the only acceptable explanation for our motivation. Philanthropy got transferred to the marketing department. Jobs for urban poor kids are justified to keep the streets quiet. Investment in formerly red-lined urban areas is done to protect our brand, our property, our growth potential in the longer run. This kind of reasoning is a measure of our cynicism.

This is the world that was handed to us. This mindset drains the life, the humanity, the soul out of us. And, ultimately, it limits our freedom, for acting on a purpose that is narrowly defined makes us smaller, less capable of independent action, even at our moment of success.

> So to act on what matters, we must choose to define our place more broadly. We do not justify it with instrumental explanations, because we are unwilling to shrink the best part of ourselves. We decide at this moment to be accountable for something larger, for the whole, for the common good, and this is a more power-ful definition of accountability. I no longer dilute my own freedom. I exchange what seems like safety for a life that matters, caring for the whole.

But how do we reconcile individual purpose with institutional purpose? Suppose you decide to care for the whole? You commit to the whole organization, even at the expense of your unit; you commit to the industry, to the community, to the environment, to creating a habitable workplace, or to a family-friendly world. If the leaders of your organization choose differently, what does this mean for you?

Nothing.

For who decides institutional purpose, or institutional values? Convention says it is top management. But why would we so easily transfer to a leader what matters most to us? The mindset that expresses Yes, our freedom, and the strength of our own capacity to take action is the thinking that *we* decide what the world around us should become. In fact, you can bet that most institutions in our lifetime will define themselves as economic or narrow-service organizations. This is their gift to us, for now we know the choices we make are our own.

Work Is a Good Place to Be

The workplaces we inhabit are perfect platforms for expressing our own intentions. My workplace is where I will find my voice. It is where I discover that I have all that I require, and because it has little more to offer me, it has lost its hold on me. It does not matter whether our organization's leadership shares our values. It is enough to hope that they share values among themselves. Leave them alone. They are not here to meet our expectations. They exist to run an organization, not us. In fact, much of what institutional leadership does today comes from what they thought we wanted and needed yesterday. It may be possible that the institution will listen to us the moment we find our voice.

Now, some rationalize their caution by saying let me play the game so I can get into the game. If I am not elected, my voice will not matter. I will sing their song today so that I may play my own composition later. This is a fool's delay. For the leaders of today had the same belief. They waited to find their own voice until they were in a position of power. At some point they looked around and discovered their time had passed, their voice misplaced. Someone put the cake out in the rain. Their desires lost their vitality from lack of use. Why do we think we will be any different?

The intent is to stay whole and maintain our own cent

Sardello, as we shall see later, writes in *Facing the Worl*

that we must bring our true selves into the world. If

operates without a center, it can cost us ours. If a com

no center, or a building shows few signs of life, somethi

within us. This is why we have a stake in urban vitality and eco-

nomic and social strength. The lack of it leaves unresolved conflict

within us. Moving to the edge of the city won't help. If we are cre-

ating the world, then it is creating us at the same time and even if

we look away, or move away, we remain eternally connected to

something larger. This we cannot escape.

▼

Citizenship means that I act as if this larger place were mine to create, while the conventional wisdom is that I cannot have responsibility without authority. That is a tired idea. Let it die in peace. I am responsible for the health of the institution and the community even though I do not control it. I can participate in creating something I do not control.

social architecture

We need a saving image or role to guide us in fulfilling our potential to create social structures that we want to inhabit. The discussion now moves to the instrumentality of our culture and how it distracts us from the pursuit of what really matters. The dominant archetypes of instrumentality are the engineer and the economist. They represent the essence of practicality and commerce. What is absent in a world dominated by the engineer and economist is the artist. The artist needs to enter our institutional experience in order to create a space for idealism, intimacy, and depth. This section offers the role and mindset of the social architect as a way of integrating the gifts of the engineer, the economist, and the artist. This is a way of thinking about what we might do to both act on our values and have an impact on how our institutions function.

12

instrumental

the instrumental imperative. The moment we gain
enough personal clarity about our intentions and decide to be accountable for bringing them into the world, we come face to face with a culture that is indifferent or even unfriendly towards the very idealism, intimacy, and depth that this requires. Modern culture is not organized to support our idealistic, intimate, and deeper desires. It is organized to reinforce instrumental behavior. But if we understand the nature of the culture, we gain some choice over it.

The Message Is the Medium

Culture is really a set of messages about how we should operate in the world. It imposes the political imperative upon each of us to get with the program, and the program requires that we become highly instrumental. The word *instrumental* captures the aspect of our lives, especially in our work, that values efficiency (the engineer) and barter, exchange, and the art of the deal (the economist). But we not only have to make the deal, we have to become the deal. Who we are gets defined as a currency according to the current rate of exchange in a marketplace. It is an accommodation we make with the world that can distract us, one degree at a time, from what matters most to us. It is the means by which the commercial version of what it means to be a person brings us under its spell.

Let us look at the word *instrument.* One definition of the word is "a person used by another to bring something about" (Webster). We are instruments to one another when we use each other for effect. This frames relationships, for example, as a means to an end, rather than an end in itself. It represents a life based on bargaining.

Instrumentalism is a philosophic stance. It is "a pragmatic doctrine that ideas are plans for action serving as instruments for adjustment to the environment and that their validity is tested by their effectiveness" (Webster again). To act on what is instrumental requires us to view the world according to how effective it is, how much leverage it can provide us, what return we receive on our investment. We begin to think of lives as instrumental rather than intimate. Idealism is a liability in an instrumental world. Intimacy is treated as self-indulgence, and there is little time for depth. If we are not careful, the values of efficiency, leverage, and return, which are hallmarks of the world of commerce, begin to become central to our identity.

What Do They Want from Me?

Becoming more instrumental not only means that we primarily value what use we are to each other, but it also leads us to live more and more according to the external expectations that are placed upon us. In this way we become a vehicle for living out the intentions of those around us—not as an act of service, but as an act of accommodation. Our task becomes adapting to our environment, which is the essence of being market driven. The marketplace mentality, which is relevant for a business, determines our identity as people. We become products measured by market value. And soon our relationships, our dreams, and even our deepest insights become a means to an end.

When we view the world instrumentally, and judge what we do according to cost and efficiency, then the question "What is the point?" is trumped by the question "What is quick and efficient?" The "What works?" question wins. "What matters?" comes in second. In this way, human values and intimate relationships run the risk of becoming the stepchildren of commercial values and operational elegance.

A Balanced Life

One symptom of our instrumentality is all the talk of wanting more balance in our lives. What do we mean when we say we want more balance between life and work? For one thing, it means that we see work and life in opposition to each other. Does this mean that we feel we are not alive at work? That our personal lives are separate from our working lives? When I am not working, it is my life, and when I am working, is it someone else's life? Is that why I call it *work*?

It is this construct of our experience that puts us off balance. In the scheme I am using here, I would suggest that it is the tension between "What matters?" and "What works?" that is out of balance. If this is true, then working at home or even spending more time with our families will not resolve the issue of work/life balance. Resolution lies in becoming more balanced between engaging in what has meaning for us and doing things that are useful and practical, or in a sense, instrumental. Being fully alive is to be in balance wherever we are.

This also can be framed as the tension between what the culture has in mind for us and what is in our own hearts. When we act on our own deeper purpose, we pay a higher price, for it often demands that we swim against the tide of the dominant culture. Until we accept the ways that the culture draws us into a life of instrumentality, we will never muster the fortitude to actually act on our heart's desires.

The Power of the Default Culture

Our institutions, and even the wider culture, operate on the belief that all that counts, all that is real, is what is tangible, touchable, measurable, and "productive." This bias in favor of utility and instrumental return infiltrates every aspect of our lives:

1. When schools face hard times, the first programs to go are classes in the arts. We can easily defend our investment in what we call the basics: reading, writing, and arithmetic. But we often treat curricula that have no obvious career potential as dispensable luxuries.

2. When land cannot be built upon, tilled, or drilled into, we claim it is worthless. I attended a zoning meeting during which the developer's lawyer said to the board, "If you do not allow us to build a house on this property the city will usurp this land and render it useless." In a world where productive use is paramount, land without commerce has no value. So much for nature.

3. Colleges today are in the business of building resumes, not wisdom. This is not just the choice of the college, it is also the choice of students. The student asks for career-building courses and the institution responds.

4. Home décor is now organized around spaces where work can be accomplished. My bed has become a desk, my dining room an office, and my family room a conference center. Eating and learning are now mobile, as my car has become a restaurant and an audiotape learning center.

5. Organizational productivity depends on externalizing and reducing human costs. We reward institutions that minimize their need for people, relocate for the sake of lower wages, and consider safety and environmental restraints as excessive government regulation.

These patterns—personal, institutional, and societal—partially gain their power through their subtlety. As powerful as the culture is, we hardly notice its effect on us. It is the sea we swim in. The culture works on us and through us and even expresses us.

In a literal sense, though, the culture does not really determine our actions or even explain why we do what we do. We are responsible for this. The culture is more like a presence in the shadows, ready to step in when we are not paying attention.

One useful way to think about it is as the *default culture*. In computer software, a whole host of default settings comes with every new program you buy. If you choose, you can change these settings to suit your preferences but if you don't, the defaults create the rules.

Each time we turn our attention away from our own intentions, we operate, in a sense, by default. In the absence of our clear intention, our willingness to consciously change the settings of the world we are creating, the default culture is decisive. This is hard to see clearly because the culture is able to absorb the rhetoric of our individuality and freedom. It (we) allows space for our own desires, it just does not encourage acting on them. While no one argues against values and desires, we fear they might lead to anarchy and chaos. The result is that although every institution lists its human values on its mission statement, these are often operationally set aside, only to be resurrected during retreats or when public declarations are required.

Inhabiting What We Create

The cultural story that I am describing is simply today's version of what is often called modernity or modernism. In *Facing the World with Soul*, Robert Sardello writes about the evolution of capitalism. He notes that in the early days,

> ... methodical, systematic, continuous pursuit of gain
> with the avoidance of all pleasure characterizes the
> original spirit of capitalism. Capitalism was born of the
> Protestant reformation. The great fear felt by all forms

> *of Puritanism is that somewhere, somehow, someone is having a good time.* (p. 83)

Or, to paraphrase, someone might be acting on their desires. The pursuit of gain, which Sardello calls "unlimited acquisition," gained respectability when it was interpreted "as rooted in human nature" (p. 85). Instead of seeing unlimited gain, or self-interest, as a choice we make, we treat it as a characteristic of human nature. And when we think of it as human nature, we stop seeking alternatives and yield to its inevitability. The economist in us gives voice and validation to this belief. Sardello acknowledges the triumph of the practical over the aesthetic and observes how fearful we are that the pursuit of desire and intimacy will undermine our economic interests:

> *... the danger arises that behavior incompatible with economy will surface the disinclination to work, an interest in art and sensual pleasure, a search for meaningful work....We keep pleasure in check, and the means to this balance is the budget. Economics becomes the management of pleasure.* (p. 85)

Interesting. The fear of capitalism is that our desires and idealism (pleasure, in Sardello's scheme) are dangerous to the economy, that we will be pleasure seeking, become artists and, worst of all, seek meaningful work. We control this "dangerous" impulse through the budget. What's more:

> *... it leads to the situation in which money itself becomes a commodity to be sought after, money doing business on its own detached from any relation to the soul of the world. The psychic starvation brought about by removing soul from the world produces insatiable greed, for when the world is no longer surrounded with soul a vast emptiness intervenes that must be filled.* (p. 86)

This is at the core of the instrumental culture. Efficiency and economic success have been culturally endowed as universal societal benefits, which we call progress. Sardello argues that this is an artificial or manufactured connection, and in fact the opposite might be more accurate. The more focused we are on economics and what he calls the "budgeting of pleasure," the greater the social cost or what he refers to as soul. He is redefining the meaning of progress, trying to move it from instrumental success to a position of more idealism and intimacy.

The Tragedy of Development

Another author who gives us a wider perspective on our culture is Marshall Berman. A professor of political theory and urbanism at City College of New York, he has written a watershed book on the origins of today's modern culture, entitled *All That Is Solid Melts into Air*. One of his insights is that although we are fully committed to reengineer, develop, and modernize our world, it does not mean this is a place we will want to live:

> *Our most creative constructions and achievements are bound to turn into prisons and whited sepulchres that we, or our children, will have to escape or transform if life is to go on.* (p. 6)

This is a way of understanding our alienation and loss of idealism and intimacy with the world: While we invest great personal energy into building a quick, convenient instrumental life, we cannot make ourselves comfortable in it.

One the most powerful stories in Berman's book is his retelling of Goethe's *Faust*, an archetypal image of our moral struggles with evil. In Berman's interpretation, Faust deals with the devil for a noble cause: economic development. He sells his soul not for personal gain, but for the sake of commerce, and becomes a developer, a person who "envisions, and strives to create, a world where personal growth and social progress can be had without significant human costs" (p. 66).

As a large development project nears completion, Faust is faced with one small parcel of land that the owners will not sell. After all attempts to persuade fail, Faust asks Mephisto, the devil, to "get the owners of the land out of the way. He does not want to see it, or to know the details of how it is done." (p. 67).

Mephisto and his "special unit" return that night and report that the work has been done. Faust is suddenly worried and wants to know what happened to the land owners. When he learns that Mephisto has killed them and burned their house, Faust claims he never said anything about hurting them.

> *Faust has been pretending not only to others but to himself that he could create a new world with clean hands...first he contracted out all the dirty work of development; now he washes his hands of the job and disavows the jobber once the work is done. It appears that the very process of development, even as it transforms a wasteland into a thriving physical and social space, recreates the wasteland inside the developer himself. This is how the tragedy of development works.* (p. 68)

Berman suggests that in the name of progress, we take little responsibility for the means of development or its social cost. His point most relevant to our discussion here is that whatever we create in the world is also recreated inside of us. If we operate in a world where efficiency, methodology, and instrumentality are the primary goals, we pursue these at the expense of depth and intimacy, and this is who we become in a larger sense. We purchase progress at the expense of our own humanity and heartfelt desires.

On the Street Where We Live

If we yield to the expectations of the default culture, we may be constructing a world we do not want to live in. To continually ask How? invites and encourages an instrumental, economy-driven culture to assert itself. The answers we receive to utilitarian questions will most often express the voice of the default culture, with all its constraints to our acting on what matters. Asking How? is inviting to dinner our own limitations and then feeling later that they were not very pleasant companions.

▼

Our willingness to act on what matters to us struggles to find its place in a world based on instrumentality. This is the work: to enjoy, yet keep in perspective, the benefits of instrumental values, for commerce and barter and practicality are essential elements of a viable economic system. At the same time, we must eventually listen to our desire to find the freedom to sustain enough idealism, intimacy, and depth so that we can act on our vision of what the world might become. Holding each of these values in one container becomes the task.

13

archetypes

the archetypes of instrumentality and desire.

Carl Jung was a psychologist who had a profound influence on our thinking about personality and behavior. He developed the concept of the collective unconscious. He understood that our way of moving through life is affected as much by the common images held by a culture as it is by individual personality and personal and family history. Central to his thinking about what drives our behavior is the existence of certain archetypes.

An archetype is an inherited way of thinking, a mythic image that exists for all members of a culture. Within the image of an archetype is collected a whole series of possibilities and qualities that helps explain who we are and who we might become. I want to use this concept of archetypes to explore a range of possibilities and qualities that help us understand our place in today's industrial-turned-information age. The instrumental aspect of the culture discussed in the last chapter is primarily given form through the archetypes of the engineer and economist.

I want to explore four archetypal images to understand what it takes for us to act on what matters: the engineer, the economist, the artist, and the architect. Each represents a strategic stance, a way of thinking, and a way of acting that brings a set of beliefs into the world. The challenge is to integrate the qualities of the engineer, the economist, the artist, and the architect into our own strategy for acting on what matters.

Let's begin with the engineer and the economist. They have forged a partnership that defines many of the beliefs that support the instrumental aspects of our culture. The dominant organizational strategies for action that we now have resulted because we turned to them to set the stage for us.

The Engineer Archetype

The engineer is the prototype of the pragmatic life. The heart and soul of an engineering strategy is to control, predict, automate, and measure the world. The engineer conceived, nurtured, and gave birth to the industrial age. The production of Gutenberg's Bible is one example of an engineering triumph that led to major social transformation.

Engineers exist to solve problems and so they care deeply about methodology and how to do it. The engineer treats every challenge as though it were amenable to a logical solution. An engineer's dream is to be dropped into a jungle with an axe and a shovel and told to create an airstrip that a plane can land on in two months. This is the engineer's idea of ecstasy.

If you can, for just a moment, imagine yourself as an engineer. What do you suppose you believe about what is important? Utility is what matters to an engineer. The engineer wants to know how things work. It was an engineer who first asked the question How? The engineer speaks in the language of installation, implementation, measurement, tools, and milestones. To be an engineer is to fall in love with your tools. To be a Zen engineer is to become your tools.

To the rest of the world a problem is something to get beyond; to the engineer, a concrete, tangible mechanical, electronic, or design problem is heaven. The engineer solves problems as a form of relaxation. Their domicile of choice is the workshop. The art form of the engineer is the blueprint. It symbolizes a commitment to what is concrete. (A foundational course in engineering education is called "Strength of Materials.") It represents a form of worship, of faith in the strength of the material world.

If you are ever angry with an engineer, discuss philosophy with them. Take them to a concert or a museum and then spend hours with them talking about their feelings and experience. Engineering is not about the world of relationships, emotions, or abstraction. Relationships, to an engineer, are something to be endured, they are at best a means to an end. A cornerstone to their strategy of change is their belief in objectivity. This is a twin desire to be right and also to circumvent what is personal and emotional. The personal is too unreliable, too easily subject to whim and fancy. It is the cause of variability and all that is out of control. This is not to say that engineers are impersonal or unemotional, just that emotions are not a domain that they wish to enter. And it is not what we want from them.

Engineering focuses on the material world and schools us in how to construct a world that can safely carry the weight of all that might stand upon it. Ask engineers about stress and they will not know you are talking about their emotional state. They will wonder how to design and construct something so that it will safely sustain two times the largest possible burden. Engineers hate risks and treat them as dangers, not as opportunities. And we should be grateful for that.

Engineers R Us

The engineer lives in each of us. It is not a job title, nor is it something we studied in college. It is an archetype, a way of thinking about the world. Engineers built the world in which we live, and so they live within us. The belief system that embraces the practical and material world embraces all the deep personal values that characterize each of us; the engineer simply represents a particular way of acting on them.

There is obviously much to recommend the field of engineering and its engineers. In fact, I've studied engineering and so hold a special affection for the engineering world. Unfortunately I studied engineering for the wrong reasons. When I entered college there was a shortage of engineers and so my family and my guidance counselor suggested this would be a field that would assure me constant employment. Sounded good to me. Engineering also offered an escape from the chaotic world of feelings and relationships. I needed a world dominated by rationality and stability. Off I went on my instrumental way and actually liked it until I got distracted by a feeling.

There is no question that an engineering strategy is indispensable to our lives. We depend on the engineer to construct the world and to make it work well and safely. Thus, the engineer is embraced as a positive and powerful image into our society and institutions.

Management as Engineer

Many of our ideas about management are an extension of the engineering point of view. Like engineering, management is about control and predictability. If you accuse an engineer of being out of control, it is an indictment, and the same is true of a manager. We expect good managers to know what is going on, to be on top of every project. There was a time when I worked for Exxon when managers were told that they should be able to answer 90% of the questions asked of them, without having to ask anyone else for an update. Managers hate surprises. The mantra of management is, "Do what you think is best, just don't surprise me." There is a downside to the no-surprise world: It makes the cultivation of discovery, learning, and risk more difficult.

Change management to an engineer-turned-manager is about clear goals, consistent practices, predictable results, and accurate measurements. This demands a clear objective, a concrete definition of the process, and a reliable tracking system. It matters less what the plan is, whether it has any larger meaning or, in the extreme, is even worth doing. They just need a plan and need to know how they are going to measure what they do. A core management-as-engineer belief is that if you cannot measure something, either it should not be undertaken or it does not exist.

The Engineering Way

Here are some highlights of the engineering archetype for achieving change and acting on what matters:

1. **Leadership articulates a clear objective.** Clear means it is about the material world. It is best when supported by people in power, for the chain of command gives needed order to the vagaries of a human, social system.

2. **Define roles and responsibilities clearly.** The engineer likes clear boundaries and wants each person's property line defined by a fence. Each job should be well defined and discrete from all others. A cross-functional world is frustrating to the engineer. Their approach to collaboration is to carefully stage the sequence of each person's involvement.

3. **Prescribe the behavior that you want.** Have a clear competency model for each job. Define the new behavior and train to those definitions. Every training event needs a clear outcome and should be able to tell the participants exactly what new tools they will leave with.

4. **Assess often and give good feedback.** Engineers invented the idea of feedback mechanisms and like to apply them to people as well as processes. The performance appraisal is a reasonable tool to the engineer, and they can see no reason why anyone would question it. The engineer is committed to the elimination of problems and so, in people matters, focuses on weaknesses and their elimination. If we want to improve quality, we need better statistically based tools.

5. **Control the emotional side of work.** An early lesson in becoming a manager is not to get too personal. "This isn't personal, this is business." For years there was a widespread belief that it was a mistake for managers to get too close to the people they managed. If we develop close relationships we may lose our objectivity, it may cloud our judgment. We keep our distance for that possible future moment when we may have to reprimand or fire someone. If we have become friends, we fear we will be unable to make that call. So we stay distant and isolated.

6. **Think of employees as one more asset.** The engineering viewpoint transforms human beings into human assets and human resources. Managers manage many assets and resources—money, technology, animals, minerals, and vegetables—and now we include people as part of this inventory. And, in case the point is not clear enough, we also talk of people as FTEs, or full-time equivalents. How many FTEs work in that department? People have joined the virtual world and are no longer the real thing, they are now equivalents.

The Limitations of Engineering

There is a price for everything, and so, too, with the engineer's view of the world. If we believe something does not exist unless we can measure it, then certain things must be put aside: love, feeling, intuition, art, philosophy. The engineer in us gets trapped by the feeling that all we are is an engineer. When you have made your way in the world as a person of practicality and reason, it is hard to put logic aside for the sake of love, feeling, and doing something for the pure experience of it, rather than its utility.

This is a characterization of the engineer as cultural archetype, not the individual engineer you may know. It is the engineer archetype that has guided our passion for what works. When we want to change or improve our world, it leads us into strategies of control and installation and is indifferent to any discussion of subjective experience. We have embraced the engineering genius and brought it into all aspects of our lives, especially our institutions. Thus, the engineering mind is key to our materialism. It does not create it, but reinforces it through valuing all that is practical and useful, and this is exactly what matters to an engineer.

The Economist Archetype

The ally of the engineer is the economist, for engineering justifies its way of thinking on the basis of cost, as well as safety, control, and predictability. We should really view the engineer and economist as a couple, joining forces to bring the values of instrumentality to bear. Where the engineer installs and measures change, the economist negotiates it on the basis of an exchange of currency. The currency can be money, or material goods; it can also be comprised of intangibles such as recognition, affection, and safety.

For our institutions, the economist creates a world where the sole purpose of a firm is to return money to its shareholders. Everything must be justified in terms of its economic return. How much does it cost? How long will it take? What will we get for it? These are the defining questions. The economist is the social scientist who creates commerce and designs financial models for everything from an individual to a business to a national economy. The economist's aptitude for model-building is of great use to us, as is the engineer's material-building capacity. What is of concern here is the economist's view of the human being. It is in this arena that we have taken their insights far beyond the pure province of economics.

The essence of the economist stance on people is that the exchange of tangible value explains human motivation and defines organizational purpose. It is the belief that barter is the means by which we get things done, deliver service, and even find love. At the simplest level, the economist believes that we are all for sale or rent, for this is the dynamic of exchangable self-interest.

If you want to act on what matters, says the economist, discover the interests of the active parties and design a plan to satisfy them accordingly. The economist believes that money, tangible rewards, or other incentives is what causes us to do what we do. My willingness to change my behavior, to support an institution, or to engage in a relationship is, fundamentally, a negotiation between what I am asked to give and what I think I can get. And I am willing to place most anything on the table if the offer is attractive enough. And if there is nothing on the table, no money, no currency, why would I sit down to begin with?

It is significant that among social scientists, economists consistently rank the lowest in any measure of altruism and social cooperation and highest in narrow self-interest and willingness to be a free rider on other people's commitments (Frank, Gilovich, and Regan, 1993). How the economists manage their personal affairs is of little interest here. What is of interest is that our culture has generally adopted the economist view of human motivation. We use an economic model to explain why people do what they do. We define for-profit organizations as primarily economic entities, and anything that does not clearly offer a return on an investment undergoes close scrutiny. We also view relationships in terms of transaction and exchange. Pure acts of charity and goodwill are viewed with skepticism, and the economist believes that the original good samaritan probably wanted something in return. Perhaps not money, but he did become rather famous.

The economist view of acting on what matters or initiating change centers on incentives:

1. **Refocus the reward system.** Begin by rewarding people for the new desired behavior. Invite the engineer to prescribe the behaviors that you want, and then put money on them. This will drive the change, for what is rewarded is the behavior that you get. People will only do what they are rewarded for. And, conversely, people will not do what is not rewarded. This leads us to change the reward system early and often. It also treats the reward system as if it is were important and vital. It affirms the belief that the priority of self-interest is in the nature of the human being.

2. **Competition is essential to success.** Whether it is students, employees, companies, or national economies, only the strong should survive. This notion is a distortion of Darwin, who found that the most adaptive creatures survive, not the strongest or the most aggressive. Our belief in competition leads us to offer large rewards for the highest performers and no rewards for low performers. The economist believes that the people who rise to the top should get the lion's share of the return. This is sometimes expressed as 20% of the people doing 80% of the work. The economist bets on the creative and entrepreneurial contribution of a small group of people who lead and direct the majority of the rest of us. The economic mindset places a premium on the act of risking capital. The major rewards go to those who put their money on the line (investors) while secondary rewards go to those who have no capital invested and who "only" do the work (wage earners). The result is to make shareholder return the number one goal.

3. **Barter is a major basis for motivation and action.** Another way of saying this is that the marketplace is the final arbiter of value. What is in demand, and the value assigned to it, is established by customers who vote with their money. This view leads us to be customer focused. It aims our efforts where there is demand and says that other-directedness is a sign of maturity and realism. It values an outside-in orientation. It questions actions that are undertaken for their own sake or investments in lost causes. It frames our actions, even our love, as a reciprocal exchange of value. The economist would never fall victim to unrequited love. It would be considered a strategic error.

4. **Apply a cost-benefit analysis to every action.** Every action should justify itself on the basis of its leverage, which is the impact it has when divided by its costs. Decisions about human values fall within this domain. We decide on levels of safety and service based, in part, on their cost structure. Institutional philanthropy becomes a marketing strategy, community development becomes a real estate decision, employee development is a business decision based on demonstrated financial returns.

5. **Grow or die.** Size matters. The larger the better. This is called progress. And it leads to the question, "How do you take it to scale?" If something cannot be replicated on a large scale, then we question whether it is worth doing at all. This places the burden of measurement on passion and desire. It also discourages us from conducting local experiments that might not apply elsewhere. The act of introducing scale into our thinking precludes many things we might otherwise choose to undertake for their own sake.

These strategies are at the core of the economist archetype. They are the elements of the way the economist thinks about change.

If you do not believe in competition, rewards, growth, leverage, and barter, you are naïve and out of touch with the real world. The final argument of the economist against pursuing meaning, freedom, and personally held values is that we should "get real." They have cornered the market on defining what is real and have convinced us that reality is instrumental.

Management as Economist

Management, according to the economist archetype, becomes an exercise in budget control, and this is the basis of power. Top level managers must have financial skills. They operate as bankers, holding us accountable for the financial promises we make. How long will it take? and How much will it cost? are the core economist-manager questions. It is not by accident that some of our most successful publications are titled *Fortune, Time,* and recently *Fast Company.* Nor is it by accident that magazines such as *Life* and *Look* have virtually disappeared. The economist questions are important, but they limit us when they become the primary questions. In recent years, high-tech companies aside, most organizations have increased their profitability through cost control. When cost and time become the very first questions, instead of just important ones, they create a culture of constraint, one in which the future is much like the past, only more efficient. Instead of creating a future, the economist, along with the engineer, focuses on predicting and controlling it.

Economists-as-managers have a great impact on human resources. Finding and retaining the best people is thought to be a financial transaction, a pricing problem. We use signing bonuses, incentive plans, and retention bonuses as our core human resources strategies. The belief that people are for sale or for rent creates a self-perpetuating cycle, wherein the more economic incentives are dangled in front of them, the more they feel entitled to them. This mindset has spread to the public sector, where we attempt to use financial incentives for educational administrators to increase student learning.

The impact of the economist-as-manager is that relationships between organizations and their members become increasingly commercialized. Employees become free agents as well as vendors, seeking the highest bidder. Employers become buyers, scanning the marketplace for independent suppliers, formerly called employees, to meet short-term requirements while offering as little commitment from the organization as possible. It happens in the name of agility, shifting marketplaces, obsolete skills, and what is required to compete in the information age.

The Cost

The economic model of the person has become so ingrained that the economist in us treads the instrumental path without really questioning it. We expect ourselves and others to operate out of self-interest. We become cynical about our institutions, and therefore about ourselves. Business school graduates focus on exit strategies as they enter the workplace. The economist mentality is not so much wrong, as it is narrow. It is this limited view of what is possible that brings into question the potential of calling, commitment, care, passion, and all the values that grow out of idealism, intimacy, and depth.

The Artist Archetype

The artist is conceived to focus on matters of the heart and is brought into the world as ballast for the engineer and the economist. I am using the term *artist* in a broad sense—I do not mean only traditional artists, such as writers, musicians, dancers, actors, painters. I want to encompass people who spend their days in the world of feelings, intuition, and the "softer" disciplines: social scientists, philosophers, therapists, social workers, educators, spiritual advisors. These are the vocations of the artist archetype.

The artist's world view ranges from indifference to contempt for utility and practicality. The artist does not really want to be accountable for the use or value of what they create. The artist can fall in love with a great idea and find meaning in the abstraction of an emotion. The artist is attracted to some things simply because they are not measurable or predictable. The artist not only refuses to seek order, but is afraid of it. Where the engineer becomes short of breath in the midst of chaos, the artist feels panic in the midst of order.

The essence of the artist is the ability to give universal meaning and depth to everyday objects in everyday life. What we consider ordinary, the artist sees with fresh eyes. Cezanne showed us that a bowl of fruit is worthy of the most detailed attention and that within that bowl of fruit was contained the landscape and form and shading of all material objects. His painting declares that our feelings, our perception—our impressions of it—are every bit as accurate and valid a statement of reality as the bowl of fruit itself. Thus, we call his art *impressionism*. Affirming an emotional world that the engineer might consider irrational or even bizarre, the artist treats intuition and nuance with respect and reminds us that a little bit of madness resides in each of us. Artists give voice to feelings, to conflict, to the prism of human experience. They ennoble uncertainty and paradox and, instead of seeing these as problems, they see them as inherent in the human condition.

The Artist's Way

The artist's pursuit of what matters centers around feeling and experience:

1. **Artists love surprise, in fact they call it creativity.** When something doesn't work, they find it somewhat interesting, much like scientists. Artists love what is unique and hope that what they create will never be replicated. The artist views predictability as a limitation and feels trapped when the world calls for repetition.

2. **Artists nurture emotion and make it the subject of their study.** Understanding what is personal and emotional is how artists do their work. The variability and nuances of life are the data of an artist's existence. An engineer sees a field and wants to do something useful with it; the artist sees a blade of grass and mourns its beauty and mortality.

3. **The artist is a permanent outsider.** The painter and the social scientist count on their ability to observe and then capture that observation in an image or in words. So they stand apart for a better view. This makes it difficult for the artist to join an organization and endure supervision. Organizations are about joint, cooperative effort. Management values team players; they put an emphasis on the rules of membership, on the willingness to sacrifice individual needs for the common good. The manager mind thinks loyalty is a very big thing. The artist sees this and stands at a distance.

4. **The artist views commerce with suspicion.** Where the economist sees commerce as our lifeblood, the artist endures the process of pricing, marketing, and commercialization. Commerce is strictly a means to an end, not purpose in itself. Artists look for others to understand and exploit the marketplace. If they become too successful too quickly, they think there must be something wrong and they need to begin again.

Thus, the strategy for the artist to act on what matters rests on the belief that if something can be clearly pictured, vividly described and shown to a waiting world, enough has been done. Transformation in an artist's mind comes from understanding and interpreting the emotional landscape, not avoiding it. Installation, a keyword to the engineer, means to the artist the process of hanging paintings in a gallery. The artist as social scientist believes that awareness leads to change, not a booby prize, unlike James Hillman, who co-authored *We've Had a Hundred Years of Psychotherapy—and the World's Getting Worse*. The artist would look back on those hundred years and exclaim, "What a great ride!" The artist's strategy of change is noticeably lacking in timetables, yardsticks, and cost controls, and this is by design, not from indifference.

Management as Artist

It is interesting to witness what happens when an artist does create or join an organization. What you have is someone who dislikes authority, who is wary of leadership and anyone who tries to exercise it. One of my first clients was the staff of a mental health clinic. Watching them agonize and complain about bosses, subordinates, and each other made me wonder whether they were in the business of curing madness or creating it. I particularly empathized with the therapist managers, for they were people who mostly saw power and authority as the root of all human suffering—and they had the power. They were ambivalent, incongruent, more cynical than their subordinates, and generally quite miserable. They wanted to be the flower and were required to be the root.

People who are ambivalent about power have a hard time using it. Some are warm and intimate tyrants, while others will not make a decision for fear of hurting someone. What redeems artists in power is that they absolutely love the drama. Most organizations composed of artists, social scientists, or academics are political nightmares. The only time there is any agreement is when someone tries to bring resolution and order to the scene—they shoot them. Artists embrace social pathology as a source of their creativity, so the dysfunctional institution is simply reaffirming grist for the mill. If you don't believe this, find me one social service agency with well-satisfied, well-managed employees, or one artists' cooperative that has made a good business decision, and I will send you a dollar. Of course, if you look and don't find one, you owe me a dollar.

For all these reasons and more, modern culture has chosen the engineer and economist archetypes over the artist. If there ever was a struggle between engineer-economist and the artist, the struggle is now over. The engineer-economist has won. Even in the not-for-profit world including government, health care, and education.

A More Perfect Union

If the doorway to acting on what matters is framed by idealism, intimacy, and depth, and the freedom these bring with them, then as much is required from the artist as from the engineer and economist. If we lose the artist, we lose a force for the reflection, doubt, surprise, and discovery that will foster what matters, even at the expense of what works. If we decide, again and again, as we must, to act on what means the most to us, then we will carry the same burden that the artist carries. The artist is marginalized by the instrumental culture, as the engineer and economist would be marginalized by an artist-dominant culture.

The tension between the engineer and artist is one reason why individual personal development rarely leads to organizational change. Personal development is about freedom, intimacy, depth, and engagement, and even though we embrace them, once we return to the marketplace, we run directly into the engineer and economist archetypes, whose basis for action is quite different. And it is the engineering belief system that is in charge. Not to say there are no exceptions, for there are, and your workplace may be one of them. But seeing clearly the engineer-artist dilemma gives us respect for the larger drama that is being played out. And remember, what takes place in the culture is a projection of what is taking place in our own hearts.

> This also offers a way of understanding why our organizational change efforts create such resistance. Most are designed with an exclusive engineering-economist mentality. We devise a vision statement from the top, set clear goals and objectives, install and drive the changes, adapt the appraisal system, enroll and reward the people who support the change. These are all legitimate tools of engineering and economy, but they lack some of the artist's instincts about learning, change, and transformation. The engineer needs the artist to bring choice, feeling, uniqueness, and passion into the process of introducing change into a living system.

The Architect Archetype

Having polarized the engineer-economist and the artist, let me suggest an image that integrates both worlds: the architect. Architects learn both the strength of their materials as well as what shape they might take to be aesthetically appealing. The architect in us cares as much about the beauty of things as their more practical properties and how to make them work. The architect does not have the luxury of the engineer to focus almost exclusively on the practical construction of the physical world. Neither does the architect have the luxury of the artist in focusing exclusively on form and the subjective aspects of the world. Architecture brings aesthetics and utility into harmony, even if reluctantly, with one another.

The goal of the architect is to begin with the engineer's question: What function or use will this serve? The design of a home, an office, a public space, or a building begins with a discussion of utility. Given this consideration, the questions then turn to feeling, ambiance, taste, and personal values. These qualities will make the place habitable to its occupants. If we create a world we do not want to inhabit, then perhaps it is because the artist was missing in its design and construction. The strategy of the architect is to bring the engineer and the artist together. The schedule, the practicality, the simplified use of a space are essential to the architect. The cost is also critical. But these are not the only points, and this is where the architect embodies the artist. The architect cares as much about the sight lines and the perspective of the future occupant. The feeling of a place is part of the language of design. The way that a building fits with its environment is another primary consideration. Color, texture, light, and other aspects of the intimate relationship between human and habitat are treated as important.

Christopher Alexander

A person who embodies the integration of structure with the experience of its inhabitants is architect Christopher Alexander. In his work, freedom and care for what animates our experience are essential elements in the construction of a building. He is the author of a series of books that create a new language— he calls it a *pattern language*—designed to bring life into structures. If you want to understand the possibilities of integrating art, engineering, and economics, read any of his books. In *A Timeless Way of Building*, his concern for building mirrors our concerns for institutions:

> *The specific patterns out of which a building or a town is made may be alive or dead. To the extent they are alive, they let our inner forces loose, and set us free; but when they are dead, they keep us locked in inner conflict. The more living patterns there are in a place—a room, a building, or a town—the more it comes to life as an entirety, the more it glows, the more it has that self-maintaining fire which is the quality without a name.* (p. x)

What Alexander calls a "quality without a name" echoes our concern for what matters—the sense of value and purpose that we bring to whatever we touch, that defines what is worth doing. His is the voice of an architect, one who is concerned with the construction of the material world. In his writing he has committed himself to create a new language for his profession. He has all the training of an engineer and has brought to that training the sensibilities of an artist. He has the qualities of all great architects, but what is more significant is that he also has given his energy to transform his profession. This is possible for each of us: To act on what matters requires us to find our unique voice and use it to summon life to the unit, the work, the institution in which we reside.

What makes Alexander an appealing embodiment of engineer-economist-artist integration is that he:

1. Cares deeply about the experience of the inhabitants of a structure, right from the first moment of design. For example, for a public housing project, which in most cities has become either an eyesore or a ghetto, he engages the occupants in the design and construction of their own homes.

2. Deems that the life- and spirit-granting properties of a building are its most important features. He declares that the expe-

rience of feelings and harmony in a room, or a building, or a neighborhood is the number one design criterion. Efficiency, mass producibility, and simplicity of construction are secondary concerns.

3. Recognizes that a building continues to grow long after it is constructed. He does not try to design monuments to immortality. Even a room expects imperfections, curves, shifts in the door and ceiling lines. Imperfection and decay are signs of life, not weaknesses in the engineering. He strives for what he calls a "quality without a name," which to some is the experience of God.

4. Has created a "pattern language," which describes the quality of a space, not just its use or dimensions. This language details the combination of elements required to bring harmony to that space. When Alexander writes about how some spaces leave us with a feeling of inner conflict because they are built of unresolved elements, elements that do not work together to create inner security, he might as well be writing about our institutions.

5. And he does this all in the context of constructing the physical world of rooms, buildings, neighborhoods, and communities. He brings his values, what matters most to him, directly into the instrumental world.

Here is a quote from another book by Alexander, *A Pattern Language*, which gives us a sense of how an architect can represent the communion between the engineer and artist. He is discussing the satisfying elements of design which he calls patterns:

> ... no pattern is an isolated entity. Each pattern can exist in the world, only to the extent that is supported by other patterns: the larger patterns in which it is

embedded, the patterns of the same size that surround it, and the smaller patterns which are embedded in it. This is a fundamental view of the world. It says that when you build a thing you cannot merely build that thing in isolation, but must also repair the world around it, and within it, so that the larger world at that one place becomes more coherent, and more whole; and the thing which you make takes its place in the web of nature, as you make it. (p. xiii)

▼

These archetypes provide images that give us insight into our inherited thinking and thereby into what compels us to act as we do. On the deepening of our own consciousness, a friend and therapist, David Eaton, speaks of the need for "saving images"—something to hold in our minds at moments of confusion and doubt. To complete the whole picture of how important a role these archetypes play in our collective efforts to act on what matters, I want to offer the image of the social architect. The social architect expands the integrating capacity of the architect into the world of cooperative effort, our institutions.

14

architect

the role of the social architect.

The work it takes to act on what matters is up to each of us as individuals. But as we do the work on ourselves, we also have to bring it into the world. My individual possibility also needs to be part of a collective possibility. One way to think of this collective aspect is through the concept of social architecture. If we can bring Christopher Alexander's philosophy of architecture into the design and creation of an organization, a social system, we can conceptualize the role of a social architect. This is someone who is equipped to act on the aesthetics, values, or intuition of a situation in the manner of the artist, and also to act on the material or concrete aspects of a situation in the manner of the economist-engineer. Adding "social" to the title of "architect" builds on the sensibilities of the architect, as discussed in the previous chapter. Instead of being so concerned with bricks, mortar, glass, and steel, the social architect is also concerned with how people are brought together to get their work done and build organizations they want to inhabit.

The Collective Possibility

The task of the social architect is to design and bring into being organizations that serve both the marketplace and the soul of the people who work within them. Where the architect designs physical space, the social architect designs social space.

The term *social architecture* has been around a long time and usually denotes a specialty devoted to designing social policy in the public sector. The role has at times been controversial, depending on your politics. For many years following the Great Depression, social architects explored an activist role for government policy to achieve social goals. Recently, the pendulum has swung and they study ways that individual and local initiatives can be fostered. I would like to put the politics of the term aside, and borrow the usefulness of its intention. Social architecture represents the intersection of care (social) and structure (architecture) and in this way it becomes part of everyone's job, especially our leaders. We might even say that the role of the social architect is to create service-oriented organizations, businesses, governments, and schools that meet their institutional objectives in a way that gives those involved the space to act on what matters to them.

The social architect is one answer to what replaces command and control. It is a role for bosses *and* employees, it is not a technical specialty. Focusing on the boss for a moment, the boss has a responsibility to fulfill the promises of the organization to its stakeholders—shareholders, board members, community, customers, and citizens. It is the rightful duty of the boss to speak for those who commission and are served by the institution. The boss also has the obligation to provide navigational insight as to how the institution keeps its promises, and this is where the social architect is required. It is the task of the social architect to bring about needed change while using methods that are based on the deeply held personal values of the members.

Matching this role to the conditions for acting on what matters, the social architect has three design criteria:

1. Is idealism encouraged?

2. Is intimacy made possible?

3. Is there the space and demand for depth?

The process is like the engineer, the economist, and the artist getting together and jointly designing a social system, where the personal, intimate, and subjective qualities of the institution are valued along with the practical, technical, and economic objectives.

Most managers intend to do just this, but they (we) find it difficult to support idealism and allow intimacy and depth into the equation. The fact that we are living in an engineer-economist dominated world creates a bias toward more control than freedom, more practicality than idealism, barter rather than intimacy, and greater speed more than depth. The choice to think of ourselves as social architects is an activist stance—radical in thinking, conservative and caring in action.

Making Space for What Matters

In addition to a leadership function, social architecture is also a role for each member as a citizen of their institution or community. In other words, all of us. To be a citizen is to show up—to accept the invitation to participate, or to create it if it is not offered, to act as a co-designer. At any moment we can choose to speak of our idealism, express our feelings, and reflect on and deepen our questions. Acting on what matters is an act of leadership, it is not dependent on the leadership of others. Thus, all of the capacities of the social architect described below are open to each of us. They represent a way to act on our values, to realize whatever strategy or model we wish to pursue. They create the space and the opportunity for ourselves and others to co-create and implement a strategy. The design work of the social architect is to bring people together to create their own future. Remember that the values that matter to us are all qualities of being alive. Recalling the earlier list:

Love	Collaboration
Freedom	Justice
Compassion	Reconciliation
Faith in a Supreme Being	Creativity
Integrity	Care for the Next Generation
Equality	

The social architect's task is to provide a context for the organization's purpose or strategy, and then engage others in a way that embodies those values in people's hearts. We may think that the task of a leader is to define those values, but that would be necessary only if there were a conflict in values, if the values worked against each other. When taken to a deep enough level and held to an idealism that believes the world is capable of living out its intention, our values can only support each other.

When we act on what matters, on our own values, we support others in doing the same. As stated earlier, when we think we have to argue about values, we are mistakenly converting those values into models or strategies. The social architect's task is to create the space for people to act on what matters to them. It requires faith in common values and interest in the common good. It is the pure economist who believes people will act out of self-interest, the pure engineer who believes that there is only one path to the future, and the pure artist who thinks that joint effort and structure is life defeating. What is required is simply the will to act as if we know enough *right now* to put the dream into action. And the belief that this is possible.

The Capacities Required

The capacities of the social architect exist all around us. They are in the hands of consultants, facilitators, and specialists in social change and learning. When these capacities are available to each of us, bosses especially, they become a means not only for us to act on what matters, but to support this in others as well. Here are some capacities essential to the role:

1. Convening

Social architecture is, fundamentally, a convening function, giving particular attention to all aspects of how people gather. The future is created as a collective act. Anyone can convene others, although the advantage of the boss as social architect is that the boss has a unique convening power. When the boss calls a meeting, we show up. When a peer, a staff person, or specialist calls a meeting, they usually have to sell us on the idea of showing up. Doable, but more difficult.

A social architect designs and arranges the room, cares about the intent, structures the interaction and dialogue, sees that doubts are made public, and focuses on capacities instead of needs. These are the tools of social change that support intimacy, dreaming, freedom, and depth.

The fundamental tenet of social architecture is that the way people gather is critical to the way the system fuctions. A culture of idealism and intimacy is not created by the decisions we make, but by the quality of the contact we make. This is why the convening power of the boss is the linchpin for creating an environment that knows what matters and acts on it.

What follows is framed in terms of a meeting, but the principles hold true for a larger strategy. Convening is a way of operating, not just a way of meeting. Here are some key elements of convening:

- **Focus on who is in the room.** What is the nature of our invitation and who needs to be in the room? This question may be the most important one because it is by being in the room that we experience the opportunity to act on what matters. Of course, regardless of whom we invite, many will not show up. The greater challenge is to devise a way so everyone is in the room when the future is being decided. Something shifts when we decide to become inclusive while answering this question, even though the answer will always be imperfect.

- **Care for the physical space of the room in which you meet.** This includes the aesthetic qualities of the room. Is there a window through which to remember nature? Do the walls display art that remind us that the room is for human occupancy? Take care when arranging the tools and furniture in the room. Make it conducive for small group discussions, for these are the basis for all social change and development— peers talking together and making commitments to each other. Don't confuse convening with speaking. Pick a room designed for lively conversation, not one designed for effective presentations.

- **Include high-interaction activities.** These will overcome isolation and passivity. We cannot act on what matters alone. People need to know who else is in the room. They need to make contact before they get into content. We are often overly concerned with the agenda and presentation and tend to neglect the power of participation.

- **Design airspace so that all voices can be heard.** Enough airtime is particularly important for the most doubtful and concerned. When doubts are expressed publicly, then commitment is possible. Remember that all doubts do not have to be answered, only heard.

- **Aim at capacities and strengths.** Make the discussion of people's gifts the focus of attention. John McKnight notes that one of the beauties of volunteer organizations is that they know how to take advantage of people's gifts, whereas what he calls "systems" are more concerned with people's limitations.

2. Naming the Question

The social architect has an obligation to define the context, or the playing field, and then define the right question, at least to start with. Picking the question is a way of naming the debate. A structural architect must work within a community's requirements, and abide by the local building codes. For a social architect, the requirements include the needs of the bankers, the customers, and the other stakeholders. While stating these requirements is the job of the leader, the architect leaves open to the occupants, or citizens, the means or the form by which compliance is achieved.

The critical task is to find the right question, one that is open-ended enough to engage everyone personally and organizationally. Instead of asking how we are going to get $5 million in cost out of a unit, ask why we are in this spot in the first place. Ask for ways that we can increase people's freedom so that better economic decisions can be made. Ask what you, the boss, or you, the citizen, are doing that increases costs. Ask how fast we should be growing. What are our limits to growth? Ask how we are depleting the resources of the community instead of sustaining them. Even ask, What is the right question? Take the six Yes questions in Chapter 2 and begin to expand on them.

The person who names the debate carries the outcome. Many of our days are spent answering too narrow a question. The social architect keeps broadening the question, for this is what engages people and creates room for idealism and depth. Staying with questions of purpose, feeling, and relationship requires postponing the How? questions, knowing that questions of methodology are in no danger of disappearing. They do not need our nurturing since they have the culture on their side.

3. Initiating New Conversations for Learning

To hold on to the intent of supporting idealism, intimacy, and depth, we need a learning strategy that is high-contact and human being–based. Technology can support relationships, but it cannot create them. To sustain the habitability of a social system we must initiate new conversations and manage the airspace so that all voices stay engaged with each other. This may seem inefficient, but acting on values that matter takes time. We change the world when we create the time and space for heartfelt, unique conversations that discuss values and affirm doubts, feelings, and intuition.

4. Sticking with Strategies of Engagement and Consent

Implied in all of this is the idea that engagement is the design tool of choice; it is how social and cultural change happens. For complex challenges, especially when we create a system that goes against the default culture, dialogue itself is part of the solution. We need to believe that conversation is an action step. It is not only a means to the end, it is also an end in itself. If we are to keep the intention and the will to live on the margin of the culture, we need to talk the implications through. If we keep the image in our minds of the artist's path joining with the engineer's path, then the future will be chosen, not mandated. Commitment and accountability cannot be sold. They have to be evoked, and evocation comes through conversation. The social architect then becomes an engagement manager: They help to decide who should be in the room at various stages and what questions they should confront, and all while keeping to the ground rule that the questions of intent and purpose precede the questions of methodology.

5. Designing Strategies That Support Local Choice

If our intent is to create social systems that people want to inhabit, then the social architect's job is to demand that the inhabitants join in designing the system. At a minimum, members can define their requirements for the dwelling place. This is needed not only in the primary construction, but each time there is an addition or subtraction as well. It may be wise for the boss to come up with a few details on how to meet those requirements, but the architect would never proceed with construction without a sign-off from the inhabitants. Some call this "participative design." It may take longer, but the alternative is to be efficient in choosing a plan that will not be supported.

Elements of Our Own Design

The substance of the design will be a combination of the models and strategies mentioned early in the book. Here are some of the design elements that are necessary to construct a social system:

1. What is the mission of the system? and Who decides this? Who are we really here to serve?

2. How do we construct the job of the leader? and Who decides this?

3. What measures have meaning to us? and Can we choose these collectively and limit their number to five?

4. What learning and training is needed? and Who decides this? Can different levels learn together in order to help overcome the social distance between levels?

5. What constitutes reasonable, transparent, just rewards? and Who decides this?

6. How do we improve quality and introduce change? and Who makes these choices?

7. How do we stay connected with our marketplace and those we are here to serve? and How does everyone get involved in doing this?

8. What is our belief system about people's motivation? and How does this fit with the values we came here to live out?

Notice that Who decides? is a part of each element. It is in answering the questions Who decides? and Who is in the room? that we take a stand on our values.

So now we have a rough outline of the social architect's role. It does not replace the need for engineers or economists, rather it is intended to enhance their strengths. The key is for us to promote activism, not to be afraid of it. These tasks of the social architect are really intended to keep technology, barter, and speed in perspective. This requires faith in our own capacities and the willingness to stop focusing on our weaknesses. Our weaknesses are here to stay, our strengths have hardly been touched. When we focus on our strengths, we confront ourselves with our freedom and other people with theirs. This is so much more powerful than the usual deficiency-oriented view which only reminds us of our boundaries.

An Example

There are many bosses who successfully act in this role. Some are well known: Max De Pree while he was at Herman Miller, and Rich Tierlink at Harley Davidson. An example of an executive who fulfills this role and uses his power with grace is Dennis Bakke, President and CEO of AES. It is not my place to tell his story or even romanticize him for the sake of making a point. I don't even know him that well, although we have shared a platform. But from what I can see, he seems to have built his business on many of the ideas being discussed here. Here are just a few indications of what he has done to fulfill his role as social architect:

1. **Support local control and local capacity.** Dennis has placed many choices as close to the work as possible. A classic example: The management of large reserve, or sinking funds, is in the hands of employee teams at each location. He wants

employees to understand the economics of the business and become financially literate. He figures that the best way to do this is to put some money in their hands.

2. **Be undeterred by failure.** When there is a failure—for example, in Dennis's case, a serious accident—and he is under pressure from both the media and his own board to pull the reins back into the center, he holds to the belief in local choice and does not change this commitment.

3. **Care for the whole.** Dennis knows he is responsible for more than a successful business; he is also accountable for the well being of the communities in which AES operates. And Dennis means it. All statements of purpose reinforce the role his business plays in the lives of those communities. He operates in countries and regions that are particularly difficult for American firms, and his business is uniquely welcomed.

4. **Be willing to be vulnerable.** Dennis admits failures and shortfalls publicly. In his annual letter to stockholders he talks about disappointments in simple, direct language. No rationalizations, no forced optimism about how this struggle was expected or key to their growth. When something did not work, he simply takes the blame and leaves it there.

5. **Value the human system first.** Dennis knows that the people who do the work are the business, not the leaders. His 2000 annual report contains no photographs of the executives, no group shots taken in the boardroom to inspire confidence. All the pictures and stories are about regular, working people. Dozens of faces looking straight into the camera, happy to be seen. Quite amazing.

6. **Name the debate.** Dennis carries idealism with him and keeps it out in front of the institution. I have heard Dennis

speak, and his idealism and faith in people is unmistakable. He seems driven to make a difference in people's lives around the world, and this is what he shows up to talk about. He also keeps the discussion of values on the table where it belongs.

When you listen to Dennis talk, you hear his modesty about his role in, and his commitment to, a set of ideals that far transcend the business. And the business has done well. The point is not this person, for by the time you read this book, all in AES may have changed, and Dennis may be leading by assigning fault and taking names. The point is that, for at least a period of time, one leader found a way to bring economics, engineering, and artistry together. If it happens only once in the world, then we know it is possible, and that it is possible for us in our own situation. And there are hundreds more like Dennis.

▼

The intent here is not to completely define the role of the social architect. Going into too much detail about this would be skating too close to another list of answers. Rather, social architecture is an image, a role for each of us to help create. My hope is that it gives some guidance as to how we might bring our willingness to act on values, on what matters, into the collective and institutional arena. The role of the social architect recognizes that acting on what matters for one person will happen in concert with those around that person. Individual effort will not be enough.

If we do not encourage others to find their own meaning, their own voice, we will never be able to sustain our own.

15

mystery

it's a mystery to me.   Part of what drives the instrumental culture and keeps us entangled in practicality is our need
for certainty. This is inevitably frustrated by the nature of human
systems. Much of what we know about how people change or
how organizations develop is based on anecdote and intuition.
The social sciences are highly social with very little science.
Much of the research in psychology has been done with college
students, since they are the only subjects that are available and
affordable. Research in living systems uses the term *research* in
the broadest terms, since it is impossible to create controlled conditions in a human operating system. One of the tenets of science is that the research be replicable, which is impossible in a
social system.

> Trying to contain human endeavors
> within the realm of certainty or sci-
> ence or engineering is both futile and
> harmful. Try as we might, we are
> unable to remove the mystery from
> life. We are constantly confronted
> with the difficulty of acting on our ide-
> alism and pursuing an unreachable
> depth, and are left with little more
> than paradox: the idea that for every
> great idea, there is an opposite idea
> that is also true.

The Problem of Freedom

The insolubility of human problems began in the Garden of Eden.
God could have let Adam and Eve remain in Paradise. But he
summoned the serpent, innocence was lost, and the rest is history. Well, kind of. At that moment we were given our freedom

and evil was created—evil in the sense that there are aspects of the world that will always be out of our control that diminish the human spirit.

It is the fact that we are free that creates unsolvable problems. The desire to see all problems as solvable is an assault on freedom. It is a belief that evil can be eradicated and that by so doing we create the false possibility that we can return to Paradise. Thus, we underestimate the power of evil and ignore the redemptive nature of the struggle.

False Certainty

Seeking certainty in human affairs breeds doubt and the belief that we are not enough. This doubt and insecurity is why we keep asking for more answers, long after the answers we have been given are unsatisfying. Seeking certainty assumes that if we knew more or knew better, we would know what to do. We would know how to end the suffering of others and our own. We think that if we were better parents, we would have happier and more successful children, or we might have gotten the children that we originally ordered. Demanding a solution, or an action plan for everything, is also arrogant. It is a wish for perfection. It is our wish to be God.

When we accept that there are sets of problems for which there are no answers, and that there never will be answers, we create room for mystery and imperfection in life. Mystery and imperfection restore our humanity. It is the imperfect room that, as for Christopher Alexander, opens us to the possibility of life. There needs to be space for wonder, gratitude, surrender, grief, and compassion in our institutional lives as well as our personal lives. It transforms what we thought were "problems" into the human condition. Our willingness to accept an imperfect and paradoxical world breaks down our detachment and creates the opportunity for a more intimate connection with the world. It helps us realize that all business is personal and thereby brings depth into our lives. And learning about questions is the potter's clay of idealism.

A Human Organization

Acknowledging the mystery of life, of human motivation, of how people make contact with each other, changes our thinking about organizational life. The diversity and imperfection of human souls is, ultimately, what makes institutions engaging, humane, and habitable. Human systems are imperfect, the homes for unsolvable problems. And we cannot take the tools and strategies of engineering and economics and apply them to the governance of organizations.

You sometimes hear the term "management science." But there is no such thing as management science, nor is there much valid social science. Even calling them "sciences" is wishful thinking. If you doubt this, let me ask you a simple question: In terms of your business, university, non-profit organization, school, hospital, or whatever your workplace, how is it going? Is it under control, predictable, and operating with reason? Or is it agonizingly polit-ical, filled with people and departments at odds with each other, struggling to live out its values and beliefs? And when you answer this question, think of people at your level and above. The only time the world looks like it is under control is when we look down at those below us. There is a vertical distortion look-ing down, much like watching the earth from an airplane. The earth looks spacious, peaceful, and very neat. Right up to the moment you land.

The Myth of Change Management

The tendency to overapply engineering and science principles to human endeavors is rampant in the arena of organizational change. For years now we have been trying to drive change. Drill down change. Roll out change programs. We want to implement and install programs. We want to prescribe the desired behavior, then train and evaluate people against it. We call them programs or processes as if they were, in fact, predictable. They aren't. If you are the recipient of these change efforts, you will see at first hand the difficulty of being the one who is driven, drilled, rolled out, installed, trained, and evaluated.

What we call change management becomes cosmetic and fashionable when we think we can predict and control it, make it into a science. There is the art of management, the practice of management, but the science of management? Not so—not if you are in the middle of it.

The work of building, managing, and then transforming human systems suffers when we focus too much on answers. The reason that we must keep going from fashion to fashion, consultant to consultant, when we keep asking How? is that we are looking for an answer that is not there. It is like looking for the fountain of youth. Don't keep looking for something you will not find. Stop digging.

The Value of the Question

What is most useful is to think carefully about the question. There is nothing so practical as a good theory, and even more so, there is nothing so practical as a good question. Those things in human affairs that offer solutions to problems float right on the surface. Human systems require depth. The deeper the better. Philosophy rather than psychology, imagination rather than engineering, exploration rather than installation. There is nothing more practical in human matters than to postpone the urge to be immediately practical.

If we can accept that there is no solution to human problems, that they cannot be engineered or purchased away, then we can accept that the question is more important than the answer. In fact, for each of us, knowing our question may be the real task. Perhaps transformation is marked by the shifting of our question.

It is in the realm of human endeavors that we will discover what matters. Here are some thoughts that are likely to lead to lasting development of effective human systems.

1. **Understand that the task is to shift the demand for the right answer to the search for the right question.** For anything that matters, the answer is in the question. Get the question right, and the answer is self-evident in every case. All that is required is to meditate, turn, and face squarely the implications of this question. Recognize that for every answer to an important question, the opposite is also true. What is the question that, if I had an answer to, would set me free?

2. **Recognize that the struggle is the solution.** Serious dialogue about the question brings its resolution. Resolution is not so much an answer, but the experience that our actions begin to shift in more productive and harmonious directions. Peter Koestenbaum says that we simply outgrow the question. It is faith in dialogue that replaces belief in formulas. The world offers you a formula to meet its needs, you answer with a deeper question that you have constructed.

3. **See the reality in the current situation.** See the suffering and the costs of what exists now. Telling the truth is a major step in any restoration effort. In this book, I have tried to articulate the instrumentality of the culture as a way of offering choice in response to it.

4. **Grieve for the costs of what exists now.** Especially for the complexity and permanence of the human condition. In facing suffering that you know is permanent, the only action that matters is grief.

5. **Gain control of the nature of the debate.** Who determines the subject of the debate? You regain control of your life by deciding what questions are important. This may not give you the outcome you are looking for, but it is a political act to decide what is discussed.

6. **Treat the conversation as an action.** It is an act of freedom to struggle with questions of identity, what matters, who we are. What do we want to become? What are our desires? Whom do we want to engage? A conversation about any of these is an action plan. It provides us with the engagement and the intimacy we seek.

7. **Raise the question of what do we want to create together, even for an established institution.** The real task is to help the institution question its own purpose. Making money and serving a constituency are too small. Acting on what matters is a question for our institutions as well as for ourselves. Meaning comes when we raise questions about purpose in our workplace—questions of social responsibility, social equity, civic engagement, the meaning the institution has for the community. All of these can be pursued while at the same time getting the work of the organization accomplished. The economists won't agree, but they have had their way for a while.

Serenading the Moon

All of these actions seem to take too long. It feels like we have been asking the big questions forever. That feeling is the resistance to going deeper and to recognizing what you are up against. The questions are too big and take too long only if you expect a final resolution.

▼

Problems that count need to be respected before they will reveal themselves to us. The focus on tools, answers, and problem solving keeps them in hiding, because we will just revert to the solutions, which are more easily implemented. The push for concrete action is exactly what sidetracks our dreams and postpones until tomorrow what needs to be addressed today. In the movie *Shakespeare in Love*, one of the characters is constantly in trouble, and when pressed to the wall on when he is going to repay his debt, he answers, "It's a mystery to me." It could be seen as a clever way of stalling, but perhaps it was a genuine expression of faith.

bibliography.

Alexander, Christopher. *A Timeless Way of Building*. New York: Oxford University Press, 1979.

———— et al. *A Pattern Language: Towns, Buildings, Construction*. New York: Oxford University Press, 1977.

Berman, Marshall. *All That Is Solid Melts into Air: The Experience of Modernity*. New York: Penguin, 1988.

Berry, Wendell. *Life Is a Miracle*. Washington, D.C.: Counterpoint Press, 2000.

Block, Peter. *Flawless Consulting: A Guide to Getting Your Expertise Used*. 2d ed. San Francisco: Jossey-Bass/Pfeiffer, 2000.

————. *Stewardship: Choosing Service over Self-Interest*. San Francisco: Berrett-Koehler, 1993.

————. *The Empowered Manager: Positive Political Skills at Work*. San Francisco: Jossey-Bass, 1987.

———— et al. *The Flawless Consulting Fieldbook and Companion: A Guide to Understanding Your Expertise*. San Francisco: Jossey-Bass/Pfeiffer, 2001.

Frank, Robert H., Thomas Gilovich, and Dennis T. Regan. "Does Studying Economics Inhibit Cooperation?" *Journal of Economic Perspectives* 7, no. 2 (Spring 1993):159–171.

Freire, Paolo. *The Pedagogy of the Oppressed*. Trans. by Myra Bergman Ramos. 30th anniv. ed. New York and London: Continuum, 2000.

Galwey, W. Timothy. *The Inner Game of Tennis*. Rev. ed. New York: Random House, 1997.

Hillman, James, and Michael Ventura. *We've Had a Hundred Years of Psychotherapy—and the World's Getting Worse*. San Francisco: HarperSanFrancisco, 1992.

Illich, Ivan. *Medical Nemesis*. New York: Pantheon, 1976.

———— et al. *Disabling Professions*. New York and London: Marion Boyars, 1987.

Koestenbaum, Peter. *Leadership: The Inner Side of Greatness—A Philosophy for Leaders*. San Francisco: Jossey-Bass, 1991.

————. *The Language of the Leadership Diamond®*. Videotape with Peter Block. Santa Monica, CA: Philosophy-in-Business, 2000.

———— and Peter Block. *Freedom and Accountability at Work: Applying Philosophical Insight to the Real World*. San Francisco: Jossey-Bass, 2001.

McKnight, John. *The Careless Society: Community and Its Counterfeits*. New York: Basic Books, 1995.

Sardello, Robert. *Facing the World with Soul*. New York: HarperCollins, 1994.

acknowledgments. This book exists as a result of the patient urging of my publisher, Steve Piersanti. He has been a helpful guide for the focus of the book and also is an executive who lives out these ideas. Acting on what matters is the essence of his publishing company. I am grateful to Allan Cohen for supporting the ideas in the book at a vulnerable time earlier in the writing.

Bernard Booms has been a great friend and also helped early on. His own care, compassion, and humanity changes everything he touches and I am always grateful for that. This is the second book of mine that Frank Basler has reviewed and his reactions are always thoughtful and from the heart. Neal Clapp also put care and thought into improving an early version, and I am always grateful for his insight and friendship. I want to also thank David Eaton, a therapist and wise human being who has influenced me in a hundred ways. He has offered me a more accepting way of looking at the human condition that I hope has leaked into this writing.

Bill Dan is a California-based sculptor who balances things in nature. Working with only his hands and a uniquely focused mental state, he painstakingly stacks rocks, glass, and other natural and found objects in gravity-defying arrangements. Clustered along a beach, a park, or other public space, his sculptures are both a meditation on form and balance as well as beautiful, if impermanent, works of art.

The photographs of Bill Dan's sculptures on the cover and throughout the book are by my brother, Jim Block, a San Francisco-based photographer specializing in portraiture for corporations, public institutions, and community non-profits. His recent documentation of architectural restoration has been published in a book entitled *A Celebration of Craftsmanship*. Upon encountering the rock sculptures of Bill Dan, Jim felt that these images would provide a fitting visual metaphor for the ideas expressed in the book.

I want to thank four more people who have made the book more accessible to the reader. Leslie Stephen is my all-time editor of choice, and she had to do double time on this book. Veronica Randall copy edited the book and did as careful and dedicated job as I have ever experienced. Rick Wilson at Berrett-Koehler has been patient and supportive in the design and production of the book, and Brad Greene, the book's designer, has given a lift to it with his adventurous spirit.

Finally, thanks to Maggie Rogers who supports me and my work in a way that makes writing possible, especially this book.

index.

about the author.

Peter Block is an author, consultant, and speaker who helped initiate the interest in empowerment and whose work now centers on ways to bring service and accountability to organizations and communities.

He is the author of several best-selling books: *Flawless Consulting: A Guide to Getting Your Expertise Used*, Second Edition (1999), *The Empowered Manager: Positive Political Skills at Work* (1987), and *Stewardship: Choosing Service over Self-Interest* (1993). *The Flawless Consulting Fieldbook and Companion: A Guide to Understanding Your Expertise*, by Peter Block and 30 Flawless Consultants, was released in November 2000. His most recent books are *Freedom and Accountability at Work: Applying Philosophic Insight to the Real World* (2001) and *The Answer to How Is Yes: Acting on What Matters* (2001).

Peter has his own consulting practice and is a partner in Designed Learning, a training company that offers consulting skills workshops. These workshops were designed by Peter to build the skills outlined in his books.

Peter has received several national awards for outstanding contributions in the field of training and development. He has served as a volunteer with the Association for Quality and Participation, Connecticut Public Television and Radio, and other local community agencies. He was a co-founder of the School for Managing and Leading Change, an intensive program to teach authentic, high-engagement strategies for changing organizations.

He can be reached at pbi@att.net. His office is in Mystic, Connecticut.

about designed learning. If you would like to further explore the ideas in this book, contact **Designed Learning**. Founded by Peter Block, **Designed Learning** is a full-service training and consulting organization existing to help organizations succeed at complex change. Through a variety of innovative ideas and technologies, we help our client organizations support the transformation of staff people into effective internal consultants and consultant teams.

The Flawless Consulting Workshops are a key element in our mission to help organizations build capacity and develop people for more successful, more meaningful work. Three hands-on, skill-building workshops are designed for internal and external consultants to learn how to establish and maintain collaborative working relations with clients, which result in positive outcomes for the business, and to learn how to have influence when you do not have control. They include:

Flawless Consulting I: Contracting

- Develop commitment.
- Work more in a partnership role.
- Negotiate more effective and enduring working agreements.
- Identify consulting phases and skills.
- Develop techniques for defining roles and responsibilities and clarifying expectations.
- Gain better use of staff expertise in the organization.
- Avoid no-win consulting situations.

Flawless Consulting II: Discovery

- Practice a data collection or discovery model.
- Conduct interviewing meetings to collect data around a business issue.
- Deal with resistance.
- Gain skills in turning recommendations into a decision to act.
- Conduct a successful feedback meeting.

- Identify methods for mapping out action steps with the client prior to implementation.

- Increase line manager commitment and action.

Flawless Consulting III: Implementation

- Choose engagement over mandate and direction.

- Create a balance between presentation and participation.

- Break away from familiar refrains to create new conversations.

- Learn the eight steps that create meetings for greater engagement.

- Handle resistance and support public dissent.

- Develop authentic dialogue within the client organization.

- Focus on assets and gifts rather than weaknesses and deficiencies.

Other Designed Learning Workshops include:

The Empowered Manager Workshop: Choosing Accountability—Making the Business Your Own

The Stewardship Workshop: Building Capacity—Creating a Culture of Accountability

The Conflict Workshop: Managing Differences and Agreement—Making Conflict Work for You

Staff Groups in the New Economy: Transitioning from Staff Function to Consulting Service

To learn more about these workshops, call us today, or visit our website at www.designedlearning.com, or contact:

Designed Learning Inc.

313 South Avenue, Suite 202

Fanwood, NJ 07023

Phone: (908) 889-0300

Email: info@designedlearning.com

Developing the Person at Work

Fax: (908) 889-4995

Website:www.designedlearning.com

Berrett-Koehler Publishers

ERRETT-KOEHLER is an independent publisher of books, periodicals, and other publications at the leading edge of new thinking and innovative practice on work, business, management, leadership, stewardship, career development, human resources, entrepreneurship, and global sustainability.

Since the company's founding in 1992, we have been committed to supporting the movement toward a more enlightened world of work by publishing books, periodicals, and other publications that help us to integrate our values with our work and work lives, and to create more humane and effective organizations.

We have chosen to focus on the areas of work, business, and organizations, because these are central elements in many people's lives today. Furthermore, the work world is going through tumultuous changes, from the decline of job security to the rise of new structures for organizing people and work. We believe that change is needed at all levels— individual, organizational, community, and global—and our publications address each of these levels.

We seek to create new lenses for understanding organizations, to legitimize topics that people care deeply about but that current business orthodoxy censors or considers secondary to bottom-line concerns, and to uncover new meaning, means, and ends for our work and work lives.

See next pages for other publications from Berrett-Koehler